CONTENTS

Chapter One: Control

Chapter Two: Accountability

Chapter Three: Impact

Introduction

Media Issues is the one hundred and forty-second volume in the *Issues* series. The aim of this series is to offer up-to-date information about important issues in our world.

Media Issues looks at media ownership and control, and the role of media in society.

The information comes from a wide variety of sources and includes:
Government reports and statistics
Newspaper reports and features
Magazine articles and surveys
Website material
Literature from lobby groups
and charitable organisations.

It is hoped that, as you read about the many aspects of the issues explored in this book, you will critically evaluate the information presented. It is important that you decide whether you are being presented with facts or opinions. Does the writer give a biased or an unbiased report? If an opinion is being expressed, do you agree with the writer?

Media Issues offers a useful starting-point for those who need convenient access to information about the many issues involved. However, it is only a starting-point. Following each article is a URL to the relevant organisation's website, which you may wish to visit for further information.

* * * * *

New media regulation and convergence

By Paul Mobbs from the GreenNet Civil Society Internet Rights Project

What is media convergence?

Multimedia digital technologies have brought huge changes, over the last ten to fifteen years, in the way that computers are used. New media (digital technologies that enable the development of the information society) play an integral role in changes within the mass media as a whole. This is known as convergence.

How does media regulation and convergence threaten civil liberties?

New digital technologies offer immense potential for civil society and it is in the interests of civil liberties that the public's rights to the use of new media should be affirmed. There are, however, political and economic pressures upon governments to restrict certain usage. In the UK the increasing consolidation of media corporations has seen a small number of players wielding huge economic power to gain control of the media market.

There is a fear that, as media converge and ownership becomes concentrated in fewer and fewer hands, the media will cease to cover issues outside the mainstream. Pressures from sponsors or advertisers could limit editors' freedom to cover issues concerning civil liberties that challenge the status quo.

There are growing restrictions on the use of new media, brought about by the increasing volume and sophistication of communications. These restrictions are of particular concern to community and minority groups as well as grassroots activists, but also affect the wider public. Some of the restrictions highlighted by such groups include:

⇨ Restrictions imposed by BT on access to the local loop (the wires that link people's home to

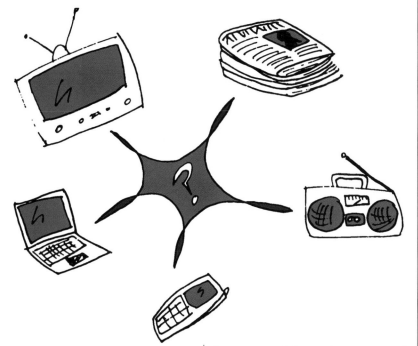

the local telephone exchange). Although the regulator (OFTEL) and European regulations require the opening up of the local loop, no efforts have been made to allow access by other service providers.

⇨ Access to higher bandwidth systems being limited mostly to urban areas.

⇨ Proprietary systems which restrict people's ability to use certain digital formats (it will be some years before free and open source systems are available for encoding and decoding of digital data, although some are in development).

Many activists believe that the Government's 2000 White Paper promised great change, but essentially took a purely commercial view of how media corporations would provide services to the public. They complain that it did not provide a framework to enable free expression within civil society, nor did it ensure that services provided by minority groups would

be protected from the actions of mainstream media organisations.

The draft Communications Bill, too, has raised serious concerns about small-scale use of networks and media technologies within the community. A small community group which sets up a network, for example, could be classed as a telecoms provider, and as a broadcaster if it then decides to stream live programmes over that network. This would involve prohibitively expensive licensing procedures which could prevent such groups from finding an outlet for expression.

Proposals for an EU Charter of Fundamental Rights Related to Technological Innovation may provide civil society groups with strategies for possible legal challenges to any legislative proposals that restrict their rights to access the new digital communications technologies. In particular the proposed right to expression provides that everyone has the right to hold, receive and impart ideas without the interference of public authorities, regardless of frontiers.

Is there an alternative model for media regulation as it affects the internet?

A number of key priorities have been identified by internet rights groups as being in the interests of civil society internet services and media groups and those who access them. These priorities seek to ensure:

⇨ that restrictions placed upon the publishing of information on the internet are no greater than those for other publishing media such as print;

⇨ a minimum charter of rights for customers of internet service providers, and to enable the establishment of a complaints procedure and of an independent body (presumably Ofcom) which could make rulings where services were arbitrarily restricted or withdrawn;

⇨ that restrictions placed on internet service providers do not restrict the ability of the public to publish material online;

⇨ that the self-regulatory approach proposed for the major broadcasters does not allow the invasion of privacy, or the misrepresentation of views, without effective means of redress for those affected by media coverage;

⇨ that the 'public service broadcasting' element of the White Paper encompasses public and community access to broadcast frequencies and internet streaming;

⇨ that the financial conditions for permits or licences for broadcasting, or the technical standards for broadcast, are not used as a means of preventing small groups or communities from setting up broadcasting or streaming services;

⇨ that the development of high bandwidth connections enables easy access to high capacity uploading (and not merely high capacity downloading through asynchronous links), so that people can develop their own peer-to-peer capacities;

⇨ that requirements for digital identities, or the protection afforded to software vendors for controlling the registration of software, do not effectively remove the ability to publish material anonymously;

⇨ that restrictions on the political content of the media are not used as a means of prohibiting small media and community broadcasters from developing their own critique of social or economic policy;

⇨ that the development of universal access encompasses access to the technologies that make the internet work, and not just the physical connection;

⇨ development of clear protection for small broadcast and online publishers or media developers against restrictive or predatory actions by larger broadcasters and media corporations; and

⇨ that the concentration of media ownership, especially cross-media ownership, does not result in greater restriction or editorial control over information or programming carried by the mass media, with a clear separation of management and editorial roles to prevent undue influence over or bias in content.

⇨ This information is from the GreenNet Civil Society Internet Rights Project. Visit www.internetrights.org.uk for more information.

© 2003 GreenNet Educational Trust

The media

Information from Channel 4 Learning

Struggle for power?

Television, radio, the internet, newspapers and magazines, adverts and music. What have the media got to do with politics? You'd be surprised. The media probably have more influence and control over our lives than anything else. They can make a government just as quickly as they can break one.

Think about it. Every day we listen to the radio, watch TV, pick up a newspaper or magazine and surf the internet. We are swamped with information. Some of it's political, some of it – but not much of it – is about politics, and politics is influenced by the media. We have a free press in the UK. Does this mean the press are free to print what they please? What might be the consequences of a completely free press?

Who's in control?

There are regulations on the media, set by the government, to prevent certain kinds of information seeping out. The media also have some influence over the government. They act as the eyes and ears of the people; they go where most people can't go. If the government puts a foot wrong or is not being entirely truthful, the media will soon let the country know.

Information frenzy

In the past, access to information from around the country and the world was mainly through newspapers and the radio. Developments in technology mean that we can now access up-to-date information at the click of a mouse.

You can probably guess that the most popular form of media is TV. It doesn't take much effort to watch it and almost every household in the UK has at least one set. This means that there is a valuable box in everyone's front room that governments can use to convey certain messages, even if you're not aware of it.

⇨ This information is reprinted with permission from the Channel 4 Learning website. Visit www.channel4learning.net for more information.

© Expresso Broadband Limited

UK media frozen out for new Potter

By Stephen Brook

JK Rowling and her publisher Bloomsbury are taking media control to new levels for the release of the latest Harry Potter book next month by not granting a single interview to an established UK journalist.

Instead the publisher, which again has threatened newspapers with legal action if they reveal details of the plot before the 16 July publication date, is bypassing the mainstream media and going straight to millions of fans to market *Harry Potter and the Half-Blood Prince*.

JK Rowling is giving 'cub reporters' aged between eight and 16 the chance to ask her questions at a special press conference coinciding with the book's worldwide release.

The cub reporters will be chosen by newspaper competitions in Britain, Ireland, Australia, Canada and New Zealand and will travel to Edinburgh Castle to gather at midnight on 15 July to hear JK Rowling read excerpts from the book.

'The cub reporters will meet JK Rowling who will give them each a signed copy of *Harry Potter and the Half-Blood Prince*,' said a posting on the author's website.

'The cub reporters will then have the weekend to read the book in a specially-created reading room at Edinburgh Castle before attending the children's press conference on Sunday 17th July to question JK Rowling in person.'

Part of the weekend will be televised, but Bloomsbury has not announced further details.

Advertising will be limited to 2,000 posters on the sides of buses, but bookshops can ask Bloomsbury for Harry Potter party packs and hold celebration parties at midnight on 15 July.

The US publisher Scholastic has coaxed Rowling to agree to a single US press interview and a single TV

'the publisher has threatened newspapers with legal action if they reveal details of the plot before the 16 July publication date'

interview while she is at Edinburgh Castle, but they will not appear until after the publication date.

Bloomsbury ran a competition to find its cub reporter by asking children to use 50 words to complete the sentence: 'I'm the biggest fan of the Harry Potter books because...', while newspapers, bookshops and libraries in the UK and the Irish Republic fashioned the giveaway into an essay-writing competition.

⇨ This article first appeared in *MediaGuardian* on 6 June 2005.

Ofcom announces guidance on media mergers public interest test

Information from Ofcom

Ofcom today set out its draft guidance on the public interest test to be applied to media mergers in the event of a request for further investigation from the Secretary of State for Trade and Industry.

Background

The Communications Act 2003 requires Ofcom to investigate matters of public interest arising from the merger of newspapers or broadcast media companies, should such an investigation be requested by the Secretary of State. Under the Communications Act, Ofcom has competition powers concurrent with the Office of Fair Trading.

Sections 375 to 389 of the Communications Act set out Ofcom's advisory obligations with regard to media mergers. Ofcom would implement the media mergers public interest test, often described as the plurality test, should the Secretary of State wish there to be further investigation of:

⇨ A proposed merger involving newspaper enterprises;

⇨ A proposed merger involving broadcasting enterprises;

⇨ A proposed merger between broadcasting enterprises and newspaper enterprises.

In the case of a newspaper merger, the public interest considerations, as defined by the Act, are:

⇨ The need for accurate presentation of news in newspapers;

⇨ The need for free expression of opinion in the newspapers involved in the merger;

⇨ The need for, to the extent that is reasonable and practicable, a sufficient plurality of views expressed in newspapers as a whole in each market for newspapers in the UK or part of the UK.

In the case of a broadcasting merger or a cross-media merger, the public interest considerations, as defined by the Act, are:

⇨ The need for there to be a sufficient plurality of persons with control of the media enterprises serving that audience in relation to every different audience in the UK or a particular area/locality of the UK;

⇨ The need for the availability throughout the UK of a wide range of broadcasting which (taken as a whole) is both of high quality and calculated to appeal to a wide variety of tastes and interests;

⇨ The need for persons carrying on media enterprises and for those with control of such enterprises to have a genuine commitment to the attainment in relation to broadcasting of the standards objectives set out in Section 319 of the Communications Act 2003 (for example, governing matters of accuracy, impartiality, harm, offence, fairness and privacy in broadcasting).

⇨ This information was released by Ofcom on 5 January 2004 . Visit www.ofcom.org.uk for more information.

© Ofcom

Parliament to decide whether media ownership has affected news

By David Rose for the Press Gazette

Parliament is to examine whether the concentration of media ownership is affecting the way journalists cover news.

An influential cross-party committee of peers is inviting evidence from the media in the inquiry, which is bound to re–examine the whole issue of self–regulation.

The House of Lords' communication committee will examine what impact the concentration of media ownership has had on the balance and diversity of opinion presented in news outlets.

The committee is chaired by a former *Times* journalist and one-time home secretary Lord Fowler who said: 'there has been an increasing concentration of ownership in the media. We want to examine if this has had an effect upon news provision. There are important public interest factors here. In a democracy it is vital to have as wide a diversity of news as possible.'

He admitted: 'There has been very little work investigating the impact of ownership on editorial priorities such as fairness, accuracy, and impartiality. It is important to know what influence ownership has in order to make informed decisions on media regulation.'

The inquiry comes only a few weeks after Tony Blair's parting swipe at the 'feral beasts' of journalism and his suggestion that new Prime Minister Gordon Brown should examine whether newspaper journalists should be brought under the same state control as broadcasters because of media convergence.

Among the issues the peers will examine will be the change in the way the news is presented, because of new technology and the way journalists are deployed.

The cross-party committee includes a former journalist and NUJ member, Lord Corbett, former defence secretary Lord King, and Liberal Democrat peer Baroness Bonham-Carter, a former BBC producer.

The inquiry will be in two parts, with the committee focusing on changes in the way people access news, developments in the way news is divided, and how contracted media ownership affects the balance and diversity of news. The committee will then go on to consider the concentration of media ownership, cross-media ownership and the regulation framework.

The government has continually supported the newspaper industry's right to regulate itself through the Press Complaints Commission, something which Blair questioned in his recent speech.

The committee's report will be presented to parliament and the government will have to respond.

> 'there has been an increasing concentration of ownership in the media. We want to examine if this has had an effect upon news provision. There are important public interest factors here. In a democracy it is vital to have as wide a diversity of news as possible.'

⇨ This article appeared in the Press Gazette on 26 June 2007. Visit www.pressgazette.co.uk for more information.

© Press Gazette

BBC funding debate

By Jemima Kiss

A BBC programme on the future and purpose of the corporation triggered a massive public response at the weekend as viewers took advantage of the BBC's online feedback system.

Broadcast last Sunday on BBC1, 'Panorama: What's the Point of the BBC?' featured a panel discussion including acting BBC director general Mark Byford, Guardian Unlimited editor-in-chief Emily Bell and David Elstein, former chief executive of C5.

More than 1,000 people posted comments to the Panorama website – five times the usual response rate. Presenter Gavin Esler also used emails from viewers to question the panel, and quoted results from a poll conducted by research firm ICM.

Most people surveyed were supportive of the BBC, with around 60 per cent of respondents agreeing that the BBC is trustworthy, good value for money and not politically biased. Sixty-eight per cent of those surveyed also agreed with the statement that 'the BBC is a national institution we should be proud of'.

However, funding methods proved more controversial with thirty six per cent stating that the corporation should be funded by subscriptions paid only by those who want to watch BBC programmes. Thirty-one per cent said that the fee should stay, and a further 31 per cent said the corporation should be funded by advertising.

Emily Bell defended the principle of the licence fee, although she felt that the last fee increase was too high; the fee is now £116 per year for every household in the UK.

'In a democracy you want as many people as possible to have as much access as they can to as broad an amount of information as possible, particularly produced by an independent news organisation,' she said.

'The licence fee should endure because it works.'

The BBC operates on the basis of a Royal Charter. This charter is due for renewal in 2006, and the government department for culture, media and sport (DCMS) is undertaking a detailed review of the corporation leading up to renewal.

A review of the BBC's online services has also been conducted over

the past few months by Philip Graf, former chief executive of the Trinity Mirror newspaper group.

David Elstein recently led a Conservative Party report outlining the party's proposals for the future of the BBC, and told the programme that funding is the corporation's biggest issue.

'The licence fee in my view is misguided. It covers both public service content and entertainment – it should fund neither,' he said.

'Taxes should pay for the first, consumers voluntarily for the second.'

Adding to the discussion on the BBC Panorama website, UK viewer Michael Nixon pointed out that people around the world enjoy BBC services although they are funded by UK licence fee payers.

'I agree that the people who watch, listen or read the BBC should pay for it. The rest of the world, who listen to online radio, or read the internet site do not pay for anything. How can that be possibly fair?' he said.

'I admit I use the site, and listen to the radio, so charge me accordingly.'

Chris Grimmette, another UK viewer, added that the BBC is great value for money.

'Why has no one mentioned the impact of the BBC's website, both nationally and worldwide?' he asked.

'The BBC can only provide such an in-depth, independent, commercial-free service because of the way it is funded. Less than £10 a month – and free for OAPs – for multiple television and radio channels of all different types plus extensive news, programme and general information on the internet.

'I think that's great value.'

Public response to the issues raised in the Panorama programme made a valuable contribution to the charter review process, said a BBC spokesperson.

'The way the BBC is funded is one of the issues that will be debated in the charter review debate,' the spokesperson told dotJournalism.

'The BBC's position remains that it believes that the licence fee is the best way to fund public service broadcasting. Subscription would change the nature of the relationship with our audience – programmes would be commissioned to drive revenues, and not because they were of public benefit.

'Similarly, access to our services would be restricted to those with low incomes.'

⇨ This article was published on 4 March 2004. It is reprinted with permission from Mousetrap Media. Visit www.journalism.co.uk for more information.

Illegal broadcasting in the UK

Information from Ofcom

Ofcom today published detailed research into illegal broadcasting – or so-called pirate radio – in the UK. The report examines levels of listening to illegal stations in Greater London, in particular the boroughs of Hackney, Haringey and Lambeth. The report also measures consumer awareness of interference to safety-of-life services and licensed broadcasters caused by illegal broadcasting.

Interference

The research found that 30% of all UK radio listeners say they have experienced some form of interference to their service. Of those, 14% believe the interference was caused by illegal broadcasters. In London, these figures rise to 40% and 27% respectively.

Almost two-thirds (64%) of all UK radio listeners turn off their radios or switch to a different station when they encounter interference. Some 2% of listeners who experience radio interference say they complain about it. This figure increases to 8% when listeners believe the interference is caused by illegal broadcasters.

The research found that six out of ten London adults surveyed were concerned when told that illegal broadcasting can cause interference and disruption to the communication systems used by safety-of-life services.

Listening

However, the report also shows that some illegal stations attract a substantial audience, with 16% of adults in Greater London regularly listening to them. Ofcom's research shows that 25% of adults in Hackney, Haringey and Lambeth regularly tune in. Some 62% of listeners in these boroughs say that illegal broadcasters offer something different from licensed commercial radio and 40% say that illegal radio is community focused.

Under the Wireless Telegraphy Act 2006, it is illegal to broadcast without a licence and under the Communications Act 2003, Ofcom is responsible for keeping spectrum free from interference. Ofcom takes illegal stations off the air by raiding studios and seizing and disconnecting transmitters and aerials. In 2006, Ofcom carried out 1,085 such operations and some 63 people were convicted of offences related to illegal broadcasting.

Illegal broadcasters transmit in the FM band. These broadcasts cause interference to the communications systems of the safety-of-life services, including the fire brigade and air traffic control, as well as legitimate licensed radio stations, such as commercial and BBC radio. There are also links between some illegal broadcasters and wider crime; Ofcom raids on studios used by illegal broadcasters have uncovered drugs and weapons.

Other key findings:

⇨ listeners to illegal broadcasters are made up of all age and social groups; however, 15–24 year-olds and C1C2 socio-economic groups are most likely to tune in;

⇨ of those listening in Hackney, Haringey and Lambeth, 55% are male and 45% are female;

⇨ listeners to illegal broadcasters in these three boroughs are from a variety of ethnic backgrounds, with black listeners making up 49% of the group;

⇨ overall, the music content of illegal stations is the main motivator for listening in London; and

⇨ nearly a quarter (24%) of people who listen to illegal stations in Hackney, Haringey and Lambeth do so because they broadcast in languages other than English.

In addition to continuing its programme of enforcement action against illegal broadcasters, Ofcom plans to consult on new ways to tackle the problem later in the year; today's research will help to inform the process.

Ofcom Chief Executive Ed Richards said: 'Ofcom's field force team works very hard to keep the radio spectrum free from interference for licensed users. However, we recognise that there is demand for content provided by illegal broadcasters in some areas of the country. This research will help shape our thinking on how to tackle this serious issue in the future.'

⇨ This information was released on 19 April 2007. It is reprinted with permission from Ofcom. Visit www.ofcom.org.uk for more information.

© Ofcom

Illegal broadcasting

The graph below details the number of operations (raids) on illegal broadcasters against the number of different stations per year since 1991 and the number of convictions in the UK

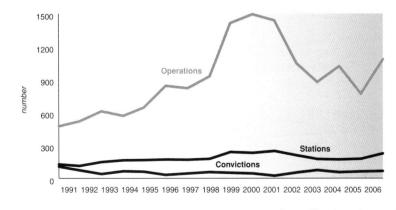

Source: Ofcom (www.ofcom.org.uk)

An introduction to newspapers in the UK

How many national newspapers? To a typical American, we're unusual in having more than just a few national newspapers. To a Frenchman, they can't understand why we don't have a national evening paper, like *Le Monde*. Read on for more information from Media UK

Introduction

Because of the small geographical area of the UK, and the good travel infrastructure, there are many national newspapers – unlike the United States, where most newspapers are printed and published locally. Unlike France, the main national papers are morning newspapers; indeed, there are no national evening titles.

UK newspapers are generally grouped into three, rather historical, groups – massmarket tabloids, or red-tops (e.g. *The Sun*), middle-market tabloids (e.g. the *Daily Mail*), and quality broadsheets (e.g. *The Times*). Unlike other European countries, there are no daily all-sport newspapers.

Tabloid? Broadsheet?

In October 2003, quality broadsheet *The Independent* began producing what it preferred to call a compact edition – tabloid-sized – along with the main broadsheet-sized newspaper. This had a stunning effect on circulation – sales went up by 20% year-on-year – and *The Times* followed suit launching its own compact edition. Both newspapers are now exclusively available in compact form.

The Guardian, which denounced the original shift to compact – before planning and then junking its own compact format – is now switching to a mid-size format between tabloid and broadsheet, known as the 'Berliner'. This format is also possibly to be used by the *Daily Telegraph*, though their ownership changes have caused a delay in their adoption.

Political leanings

The two most popular newspapers are *The Sun* and *The Daily Mirror*. Bitter rivals, the papers until recently held very differing political views – *The Sun* being Conservative (right-wing) since the early 70s, while *The Mirror* being Labour (left-wing). Both now appear to support Labour. Historically, *The Sun* appears to support the current government.

Sex!

With the mass-market tabloids, just as in other areas of life, sex sells. *The Sun* is home of the famous Page Three girl – an idea used by *The Mirror* for a while, but dumped in the 1980s. *The Daily Star*, a sister paper for the *Daily Express* (originally launched to use spare capacity in the *Express* printing presses), gives its readers regular 'StarBirds' throughout its pages and the advertising catch-phrase 'Oooh Ahhh Daily Star' (and is, incidentally, a relative success in comparison to the Express). A relative newcomer, the Manchester-based Daily Sport, is closely linked with the pornography industry, and consists mainly of a diet of fanciful stories, any stories or trials connected to sex.

Middle-market tabloids

The middle-market tabloids, the *Daily Mail* and the *Daily Express* are (possibly thankfully) concerned with a very different readership – that of affluent women. Weekend supplements and carefully–placed sponsorship ensure that these titles are a cheap alternative to a magazine, while sports supplements aimed at the husband aim to broaden their readership. The *Daily Mail* has a staunch right-wing agenda, and is lampooned by some for their over-alarmist headlines, particularly about political asylum seekers. However, its formula, said by former owner Lord Northcliffe to give his readers a 'daily hate', has made the *Daily Mail* one of the most popular newspapers in the UK.

The quality broadsheets – and quality compacts

The broadsheets are probably the most famous to readers overseas. *The Times*, the UK's oldest national newspaper, is not the most popular – that accolade falls to the *Daily Telegraph*, known affectionately as the Daily Torygraph because of the staunch support to the Conservative Party. *The Independent* and *The Guardian*, together with financial newspaper *The Financial Times* (which, incidentally, is not related to *The Times* in any way), make up the rest of the broadsheets. It's important to notice, though, that the mass-market tabloids sell up to four times as many copies as the broadsheets – and if you're looking in vain for 'The London Times', such a newspaper title has never, in fact, existed – *The Times* has always been a national newspaper. *The Guardian*, once based in Manchester, was known as *The Manchester Guardian* until the 60s.

The Fleet Street revolution

Newspaper publishing in the UK underwent a revolution in the mid 1980s, fuelled by the launch of Eddie Shah's middle-market *Today* newspaper. Freed of the out-dated practices of the print unions, this, the UK's first colour newspaper, threatened the established newspapers by using computers almost exclusively to typeset and print the paper. In this way, a newspaper could survive with a far lower readership, because it was simply cheaper to produce. The launch was not without its faults – problems with colour printing led to the title being lampooned on the satirical TV programme *Spitting Image* as being printed in 'Shah-vision', while the first edition's front page, a full-colour picture of the Queen on tour abroad, was nearly two hours late, making distribution of the paper a nightmare. The middle-market *Today* wasn't a hit with advertisers and conservative readers, and, swallowed by Murdoch's News International empire within two years, it was closed in 1995. However, its legacy lives on to this day.

Fleet Street in London, for years the home of the British press, is now deserted by publishers. The revolution in work practices coincided with expansion in the once-derelict East London Docklands, reinvented as a centre for business. News International titles *The Times* and *The Sun* moved to purpose-built buildings in Wapping, in the East End of London. The 're-engineering' of the titles' production was acrimonious, with many people being made redundant; the Wapping plant was picketed for a long while afterwards. *The Daily Telegraph*, along with *The Independent* and *The Mirror*, moved into Canary Wharf (properly known as 1 Canada Square), the centre-piece of the Docklands and one of the highest buildings in the world.

A trip down Fleet Street these days is still worthwhile; the art-deco *Express* building still stands, and is a shining example of 1920s architecture. Near it is the old *Daily Telegraph* building, still suitably adorned with its former owner's name, and still also including the alleyway to Peterborough Court, the place that gave its name to the recently-disappeared humorous gossip column in the paper.

The free newspapers

A relatively recent phenomenon in the newspaper industry has been the free morning papers. Free weekly papers are fairly common, supported by advertising and carrying little in the way of editorial. But now, with the launch of Associated's *Metro* in London, Birmingham and Leeds, a sister paper called *News* in Manchester, plus Manchester's own *Metro News* and similar titles in Tyneside, Edinburgh and Glasgow, these newspapers thrive on public transport and in busy cities. Giving editorial almost as good as the paid-for dailies, are these a threat to the established titles?

The Metro is a canny operation – in London, it's deliberately difficult to get hold of a *Metro* after 9.00am, to avoid causing sales problems with Associated's *Evening Standard* later in the day. In the author's tube station, supplies run out at around 7.50am. In late 2004 the *Evening Standard* itself joined the free newspaper revolution with the launch of Standard Lite, a cut–down free edition available at lunchtime in London.

The Guardian Media Group's *Manchester Evening News*, who launched their own spoiler free morning paper in late 1999 (called, ironically, *Metro News*), launched a free lunchtime paper in March 2005 with the launch of *MEN Lite*.

The future

Consolidation seems one of the ways forward. *The Times* and *The Sun*'s parent company also owns Sky television, the UK's satellite television service. The *Guardian* group now owns the Smooth FM and Real Radio radio stations, as well as probably the biggest internet presence for a newspaper. On a local scale, the *Kent Messenger* group also owns the local KMfm radio stations in many areas of Kent, and agressively cross-promotes them.

New sizes and formats may arrest the decline of newspaper buying. In June 2004, newspaper sales were declining year-by-year by 4.7% – the only increases worldwide, in fact, coming in developing countries. However, reductions in size for some of the newspapers have meant an increase in circulation, albeit arguably a temporary one. And, while newspaper sales have been slowly declining, consumption of news can be claimed to have vastly increased: whether from the internet, or one of the eight non-stop news channels available to UK viewers.

Newspaper companies own content. The best way of consumption of this content at present is on small sheets of dead, pulped, reformed, wood. It requires no recharging; losing a newspaper is not a major problem; and delivery and availablity is easy. However, some newspapers are experimenting in delivery of the printed newspaper by the internet – you download a PDF instead of picking up a printed paper. All national papers now have their own websites; some are shifting classified advertising away from the printed paper. Content is a useful commodity – and the way this is presented in the future may well change. The cleverest newspapers will adapt to use their content in different ways.

⇨ This information is reprinted with permission from Media UK. Visit www.mediauk.com for more information.

© MediaUK

Using the media

'The only chance you have of reaching people who haven't yet heard what you've got to say is through the media.' George Monbiot outlines some lessons in media manipulation for activists

You might, with good reason, regard the papers and broadcasters with extreme suspicion, but the struggle to make a change in the world as much as anything else is an 'information war'. You need to learn how to exploit the media before the media exploit you.

What we're up against

A. *Triviality*

Every media outlet shares the same principal aim: to expand its share of the market. It does this by seeking to grab and hold onto people's attention. This is why the media concentrates so much on events rather than issues, and especially trivial, flashy and colourful events. Most journalists are convinced that people can't concentrate for more than a few seconds. This is mainly because they can't concentrate for more than a few seconds.

On the face of it, this is a major disadvantage for us, as our aim is to make people aware of big and important issues.

B. *Bias*

Many outlets have a secondary aim: of pandering to the prejudices of their proprietors. As most large news–gathering organisations are run by perverse billionaires whose interests are at odds with those of the rest of society, this makes life still harder for us.

In practice, it means that there are some outlets we, as activists, simply have to avoid: there's no point in approaching *The Sun*, for example, unless you're appealing to narrow nationalism or are prepared to get your tits out. Stay well away from the *Daily Mail*, unless you're highlighting an animal rights issue which doesn't involve a confrontation with big business/landowners/hunters etc.

But there are often a surprising number of opportunities for making use of other parts of the right-wing

media: some of the things that occasionally slip past the editors' noses at the *Telegraph* and *Sunday Telegraph*, for example, are pretty unexpected. While their editors and proprietors may be total bastards, a lot of journalists are not bad people, just weak and cowardly. Many of them want to help, and will look for opportunities to do so without upsetting their bosses.

Newspapers are allowed to be partisan, and expected to be by their readers. But the broadcast media are legally obliged to be balanced and fair. In practice, as we know, this isn't always the case, and there are certain programmes that you should avoid at all costs. More importantly, their concept of fairness is a narrow one: as long as both Labour and Tory politicians have had their say, balance is seen to have been achieved, even if the view from Westminster represents just a tiny part of the political spectrum.

Most broadcast outlets are also very conscious of the views of their advertisers, and even more trashy than the printed ones. The result is, once again, conservatism: broadcast journalists appear to be terrified of telling their audience something it doesn't know already.

C. *The Game*

Another way in which we're up against it is that we take our campaigns seriously, while interviewers tend to see their work as a game, whose political outcome is immaterial, but

which must be played by a set of rules. These rules are, at first sight, obscure to people without a lot of media experience. If you don't play by the rules, it's a foul and you're sent off. As our only objective is to win, regardless of etiquette, we tend to foul more often than other contributors. As a result, sometimes we come across very badly.

That's the bad news, but there's also plenty of good news: we have several significant advantages over our opponents.

Our advantages

A. *Integrity*

We're genuine people, not hired hands defending a corporate or institutional position. This shows when we allow it to: an open and straightforward appeal to commonsense can cut through the clamour of self-interest and spin-doctoring with a powerful resonance. When we keep our message uncluttered and get straight to the point, we can be devastatingly effective.

B. *Articulating public sentiment*

People are increasingly prepared to listen to what we have to say: many know in their heart of hearts that things are going badly wrong, and could be very much better. Activists in the media have often been able to reach parts of the public psyche that no one else can touch, as they articulate sentiments that have never been put into words before. Hard as it may be to believe, a lot of mainstream journalists are secretly sympathetic to the causes we espouse.

C. *Inherent media friendliness*

We're colourful, fun, outlandish and outrageous. Much as television executives might claim to hate us, television cameras love us.

⇨ This information is reprinted with permission from YouthNet. Visit www.thesite.org for more information.

© *YouthNet*

Talking to journalists

A guide for young people, by Professor Mike Jempson from Media Wise

First things first

Always find out WHO you are talking to before you agree to an interview. Journalists should carry some form of identity. Ask for a copy of their 'card' which should have their contact details, who they work for, etc. This could be very important, especially if you want to find out how they have used the interview – or if you need to make a complaint about their behaviour.

Journalists should seek permission from an appropriate adult (parent/ guardian/ teacher/supervisor) before interviewing OR taking pictures of a child or young person (under 16).

The reporter's job is to ask questions, but you are NOT obliged to answer them, especially if it involves revealing personal information you would prefer to keep private.

If at any time you feel uneasy about the person conducting the interview, or the questions they are asking, just say politely that you do not want to continue. That is your right.

You may be able to make general comments about what you know about how other children think about things, but do not answer specific personal questions about other children.

Do not give reporters your personal contact details; it is best to ask them to contact you through an adult (parent/guardian/teacher/youth worker, etc.).

Some things to think about

Today the media are global – newspapers, radio and TV programmes can be accessed anywhere in the world through the internet. When you talk to a journalist you have to understand that you are talking to the world. Your story may not reach everybody in every country, but you can be sure that it will reach further than you can imagine.

You may think you WANT to talk about your story NOW, but later you may regret it. Ask yourself:

⇨ How would your friends and family react if your story is published?

Media Wise... for better journalism

⇨ Can you guarantee that your story will be not be seen by people whom you do not want to know about it?

⇨ Are there people you need to protect when telling your story – friends, people who have been kind to you?

⇨ Are there people who might want to harm you if they saw your story?

Try to imagine how you would feel if your children were to read your story in a few years' time.

Be prepared

If you are planning to share your ideas with the rest of the world, the best way is to do it is to get some sympathetic media coverage. But if you are going to talk to journalists, it is best to understand first what they want from you. Their job is to introduce and explain things to the public, NOT JUST TO GIVE YOU PUBLICITY.

Often they have a limited time in which to complete their work. Don't let them rush you, but do try to understand that they may be working to tight 'deadlines'.

Journalists work for all sorts of different media outlets – radio, television, and the internet as well as newspapers and magazines – and with different audiences in mind – young people, parents, politicians, special interest groups etc. It is a good idea to ask journalists who their audience will be, then you can try to talk about things that are likely to interest them.

Newspapers and magazines want 'good stories' that will interest their readers, many of whom may be much older than you, and with different interests.

Radio journalists want good clear voices, and television wants 'good pictures' as well as stories that will interest the viewers and listeners.

If you are being interviewed for a NEWS programme, very little of what you say will be broadcast, so try and think of simple statements ('sound bites') that make your main points. For example: 'Most adults don't seem to understand that children have rights, but we know we have rights. We are not asking much – just the same things that adults take for granted.'

Before you talk to journalists, the

first thing to do is to know what you want to say. Think about the two or three MAIN POINTS you want to make. Do not be afraid to repeat them in different ways.

One of the best ways is to tell a little story that illustrates your point. This can conjure up an image in people's minds which they will remember (and it should give the journalists ideas about how to illustrate your contribution).

For example: if there is no safe place for young people to meet up in your area, you could say just that, but it will be more powerful if you can describe an accident that happened because children were playing on unsafe waste ground or buildings, or how the police are called when young people meet up in a group on the street. Explain how it FEELS to be unwelcome in your own neighbourhood.

Talking about sensitive issues

You may be asked for an interview about a sensitive issue – about family matters, your personal circumstances, sexual matters, about a crime, or about war.

You should not normally agree to be interviewed about such things unless and until you know exactly how the interview is to be used (for what newspaper, magazine or programme; in what country and for what audiences).

Your wellbeing is more important than anything a journalist wants to ask you.

It may be very important to ensure that your full identity is not revealed. Journalists will need to know that

they are talking to someone who is genuine, so they will need some information (like your real name) to help them check facts and assure themselves that you are not just making things up. So you both have to build a relationship of trust.

If your identity is an issue, you MUST obtain an assurance from the journalist, preferably in the presence of, or through, an adult you trust that your identity will be protected. Do you want your picture to be published? If you are anxious about it, either say NO to being photographed, or seek an assurance that you cannot be identified from any picture that does appear. Obtain an agreement that the journalist will give you an 'assumed name' or just a set of initials (which need not be your own – in some countries it is the custom only to use a child's initials).

Before you take part in the interview, discuss with a sympathetic adult and tell the journalist:
⇨ what you are prepared to talk about;
⇨ what you are NOT prepared to talk about;
⇨ what YOU want to say;
⇨ whether you want an appropriate adult to be with you for the interview.

If the journalist will not agree to your terms, do not take part in the interview.

If you go ahead with the interview you must TELL THE TRUTH. Lying to journalists is very unwise. If they discover you are lying they may not believe other things that are true. You will have betrayed their trust so they might betray yours.

Press Conferences

If you are taking part in a major event or campaign, you may be asked to take part in a press conference.

Usually the main speakers will be on a stage with the journalists, sitting in rows in front of them, and photographers and camera operators moving around the room to get the best pictures.

The most important part of a press conference is when the journalists start asking questions after the main speeches. They want good answers they can use in their reports. Try to work out what questions they are likely to ask YOU, and have some short, simple answers ready. The other (adult) speakers should have some ideas about this, so it is important to meet with them and discuss

If you are to be a main speaker, prepare a short speech in advance which makes all the main points you want to communicate. It should also explain who you are and why you are involved. Copies of your speech may be given to journalists so this is a very important document.

Sometimes journalists can be rather 'patronising' when dealing with young people at a press conference. Do not let this upset you, or trick you into giving 'cute' or 'childish' replies. You are there to speak your mind, just like the adults present. Say what YOU want to say.

If you are representing an organisation your job is to communicate that organisation's message. That does not prevent you from expressing a personal viewpoint, but you should make clear when you are speaking for yourself rather than the organisation.

Ten top tips
⇨ Dress smartly but comfortably, so you do not feel awkward when you get up to speak.
⇨ Go to the toilet before you go on stage.
⇨ Make sure a glass of water has been provided for you. If you are nervous your mouth might get dry, but only take sips of the water when you need to.
⇨ Make sure you have a pad of paper and a pencil (as well as your speech). You might want to

make notes about things that are said, figures that people quote, or questions that are asked. It could help you answer questions later.

⇨ Use the microphone if one is provided, especially if the event is being recorded.

⇨ Do not be distracted by your surroundings. Pay attention to what others are saying. It is a good idea to look at whoever is speaking at the time.

⇨ Always be polite, but stand up for yourself if someone tries to put you down or get a laugh at your expense.

⇨ If you are appearing in public before the press, you may be asked for an interview after the main business is over. Let the organisers know if you are willing to do this.

⇨ Collect cards from any journalist who speaks to you – they might be useful later.

⇨ Do not give out your personal details (home or email address or telephone number). Tell anyone who asks for them to contact you through the organisers.

Recorded radio interviews

Radio journalists may want to record an interview with you for use later, perhaps in several different ways (for a news broadcast or a 'magazine' programme).

The interview will be much longer than the material that is eventually broadcast. It will be edited later, that means you can make a few mistakes, ask for a question to be repeated, or stop for a break.

However, it also means that what you say may not be used in its original context, or may even be edited to suggest things that you did not mean to say.

Always ask how the interview is going to be used, who the expected audience will be, and when it will be broadcast – so you can check that your words have been used correctly. Do not be afraid to complain if your interview is misused.

Before the interview starts ask what questions the reporter will begin with. A good interviewer will have some prepared questions, but will then ask questions that arise from what you have been saying.

When s/he is ready to start the reporter will ask you to say a few words into the 'mic' to check voice levels and make sure you can be heard distinctly and evenly.

Once any adjustments have been made try not to move away from the 'mic' and try to keep your voice level constant – don't suddenly shout or start whispering. This will make it easier to edit the tape later.

⇨ Be friendly in your responses and put a smile into your voice – think of it as a conversation with all the listeners, and no one likes to be lectured.

⇨ Try to avoid long and complicated answers – they may be edited out, or if only parts of your answer is left in, your message may be misrepresented.

⇨ Try to avoid jargon and abbreviations – if you do the interviewer may have to interrupt to ask you to explain what you are talking about, and then you could lose track of what you wanted to say.

⇨ If you make a mistake, or are unhappy about something you have said STOP – cough, laugh or simply say 'I'm sorry, can we do that again?' The reporter will understand. S/he will want you to perform well, so s/he gets a good uninterrupted interview.

⇨ When the interview is over ask to hear some of the recording, or ask the reporter for some tips about how it went. Remind the reporter of the parts you thought were important. S/he may edit the tape but may not have full editorial control over how it will be used. S/he will let the editor or producer know about the best bits.

Live interviews in a radio studio

Radio studios sometimes feel strange. They are sound-proofed and may have no windows to the outside world.

The best way to deal with studio nerves is to be familiar with your surroundings. If you are hoping to do a lot of broadcasting, get to know your local radio station. Most local radio stations welcome visits from their listeners – arrange to go on a tour with friends, your school or youth club.

If you are asked to go into the studio for an interview:

Make sure you arrive on time (some radio stations may even send a car for you if you do not have transport).

Go to the toilet before you get into the studio itself.

Ask for a drink of water if you are feeling nervous – but if your mouth gets dry, sip it.

⇨ Greet the presenter if s/he is not 'on air' but otherwise don't speak unless spoken to – the 'mic' might be on. You may be asked to wear headphones so that you can hear the programme as it is broadcast.

⇨ The presenter may have a chat about how s/he intends to handle the interview, so don't forget to ask what the first question will be.

⇨ S/he will have been given a brief note about who you are and why you are there, but may have no idea what you are going to say. If s/he says something about you that is not correct, do not be afraid to put it right if it is important to you.

⇨ When the interview starts, put a smile in your voice, take a deep breath and try to RELAX.

⇨ Most listeners are unlikely to know much about you – so try to explain things simply. Put lots of expression into your voice. If you use words (adult) listeners may not understand, your interviewer may interrupt to ask you to explain.

⇨ Try to keep talking, but watch for signals from the interviewer. S/he may interrupt you if you are going on too long and s/he wants to ask another question to keep listeners interested.

⇨ If you 'dry up' don't worry. The interviewer will take over – there is nothing worse than silence on the radio.

⇨ Try to remain calm and polite, as in a way you are representing young people.

⇨ Do not use bad language, or be too rude about people. It can upset listeners and you may say things which could result in complaints, which may loose you support.

Going on television

If are invited to appear on television, make sure you know what type of programme it will be. Ask the researcher or journalist what questions you are likely to be asked, and think carefully about the points you want to make or the messages you want to communicate.

Television is all about images, so even what you wear and how you conduct yourself will convey a message to the audience. First impressions are very important, so dress to suit the occasion in comfortable clothes. If you want people to listen to you, remember that viewers are easily distracted by unusual fashions, clashing colours and jangling jewellery.

Go to the toilet before the programme starts. You may be in the studio for some time. It may also be hot under the studio lights. If you are taking part in a formal interview ask for a glass of water to be provided and sip it only when you really need to.

Take along some simple notes to remind you of numbers or addresses or documents you want to quote. Don't shuffle your papers. Glance at them when you need to.

As the countdown starts, take a deep breath and try to be calm. Sit up, sit still, and adopt a friendly attitude. If you are sitting up at a table, place your arms on it and lean forward slightly. If you are in an easy chair, either sit yourself back in the chair and as upright as possible, or sit as comfortably as you can on the edge.

Give a positive and confident 'hello' if the presenter welcomes you. S/he will want to make you feel at home. Try to keep a smile in your eyes and your voice.

You know what you want to say, so be confident but not bossy. Remember you are in conversation with the audience through the presenter, whose job it is to ask the questions s/he thinks the public want answered. Direct your answers to the person who asks the questions, and try to ignore the cameras.

Show other guests respect; watch them with interest when they are speaking. The audience at home will be watching your reactions, and you don't win arguments by being rude. If there is a studio audience, show pleasure if you get a laugh or applause, but remember that it is even more important to impress the audience at home.

Don't be afraid to stand up for yourself if the questioning gets hostile, but don't lose your cool. The camera magnifies your mood – so avoid angry outbursts and bad language. Speak your mind, but be careful about what you say. Do not accuse people directly of lying or of criminal activity, for instance. Say things like 'I think you have got that wrong' or 'I don't agree', or just describe truthfully what happened to you. The laws about defamation (libel) and contempt of court apply to you and the television company.

If you are taking part in a studio debate, don't watch the monitors. Keep alert and take an interest in what others are saying even when you think you are not on camera. The people in the control room will be able to see you all the time, and the cameras may pick you out if you start yawning, or fiddling.

Signal to the presenter when you want to speak, but watch out for the floor manager, who will signal to the presenter when time is running out. Try to get in with a final point. Remember, the last word always leaves a lasting impression.

⇨ This information is reprinted with permission from MediaWise. Visit www.mediawise.org.uk for more information.

© MediaWise

How can young people get their voices heard more in the media?

We recently had a bash at the House of Commons to launch a report all about how young people feel they're represented by the media and politicians. Here's what the young peeps there told us

Getting young voices heard.

forum for old people and young people to chat together.

Kate, 20
I think something that is largely underestimated is writing to the newspapers. It's often seen as something that 'disgusted' of Tunbridge Wells does and not you; but if young people do begin to write to both local and national papers they'll begin to make the editors and the journalists aware that they do have views and they aren't afraid to express them. Hopefully this would encourage them to come back and begin to consult with young people and start a two-way dialogue.

Muhammed, 19
We can encourage young people to write in the local newspapers and local youth magazines and encourage them to write young people's stories which will encourage other young people to do the same.

Rachael, 20
I – and other young people – can talk to the media, write letters to the local newspapers, go to television talk shows, just basically get our voice out there into the media, do it everywhere, get published. If you've done something good or if you do something voluntary write to the local newspaper because that's the only way the media are going to find out, if we let them know what we are doing. Young people are sort of doing this but they don't realise they can approach the media rather than waiting for them to make the first move.

Sophie, 19
I find there are plenty of opportunities if you look for them. Online media is the most accessible for young people I think, and plenty of us have our own blogs, but if you're not interested in all that hassle then you could join somebody else's. The broadsheets have them and if you care to comment on them I think that would be a good

Emma, 19
It's partly our responsibility to raise our voices and actually use the vehicles that are already open to us, like writing to newspapers or doing flagship events where the media is going to come along and take a look at what you're doing. It's also about the media taking responsibility to actually listen and go out there and try and dig out the views of young people. Especially those who are less active, but still have opinions, and are just less aware of the vehicles that are available to them.

Emily, 23
I think all young people have a responsibility to be involved in politics whether they realise it or not. Even if they are not of the age to vote they've got a responsibility to be actively involved in politics, by writing to their MP and discussing issues of other young people that affect them directly. I think this applies to the press as well – if we keep targeting them we are going to make a difference.

Katie, 17
Young people should carry on working to fulfil their individual potential, so when they do get asked their opinions by politicians and the media they've got well-prepared answers and they can show who they really are. It sounds cheesy but it's true!

⇨ This information is reprinted with permission from YouthNet. Visit www.thesite.org for more information.

© YouthNet

Blair backs new online journalism register

By George Jones

Tony Blair hinted today at new restrictions on internet journalism, saying online news coverage had become 'more pernicious and less balanced' than traditional political reporting.

In a farewell lecture on public life, he said that much of the British media behaved like a 'feral beast, just tearing people and reputations to bits'.

But he had particularly harsh words for non-traditional media outlets, particularly the internet.

'It used to be thought – and I include myself in this – that help was on the horizon,' he said.

'New forms of communication would provide new outlets to by-pass the increasingly shrill tenor of the traditional media.

'In fact, the new forms can be even more pernicious, less balanced, more intent on the latest conspiracy theory multiplied by five.'

The emergence of internet-based news and 24-hour television news channels meant reports were 'driven by impact'. He said that there was a need for the distinction between news and comment to be reasserted.

With newspapers increasingly moving online, he said the regulatory systems for papers and TV needed to be revised. Currently they are monitored by separate watchdogs.

'As the technology blurs the distinction between papers and television, it becomes increasingly irrational to have different systems of accountability based on technology that no longer can be differentiated in the old way,' Mr Blair said.

The outgoing Prime Minister said senior figures in public life had now become 'totally demoralised' by the completely unbalanced nature of reporting.

He conceded that relations had always been fraught, but said the situation now threatened politicians' 'capacity to take the right decisions for the country'.

TONY BLAIR'S IDEAL MEDIA:
FAIR AND BALANCED
STATUS QUO
POLITE
RESPECTABLE
UNBIASED

THE "FERAL BEAST":
QUESTIONS AUTHORITY
INDEPENDENT
IRREVERENT
INVESTIGATIVE
RUDE

The Prime Minister acknowledged that he had 'contributed' to the deteriorating situation with the media by 'spinning' too much in the early days of New Labour.

'We paid inordinate attention in the early days of New Labour to courting, assuaging, and persuading the media,' Mr Blair said in a speech to Reuters.

'In our own defence, after 18 years of opposition and the, at times, ferocious hostility of parts of the media, it was hard to see any alternative.

'But such an attitude ran the risk of fuelling the trends in communications that I am about to question.'

While insisting that he was not complaining about the coverage he gets as Premier, Mr Blair claimed there was less balance in journalism now than 10 years ago.

Mr Blair insisted that there was still a genuine desire for impartial news coverage among the public.

'At present, we are all being dragged down by the way media and public life interact,' Mr Blair said. 'I do believe this relationship between public life and media is now damaged in a manner that requires repair.

'The damage saps the country's confidence and self-belief; it undermines its assessment of itself, its institutions; and above all, it reduces our capacity to take the right decisions, in the right spirit for our future.'

⇨ This article first appeared in the *Telegraph* on 13 June 2007.

Regional papers making good use of FOI, report shows

Regional newspapers are making good use of the Freedom of Information Act and unearthing stories on a wide variety of subjects, according to a new report published by the Campaign for Freedom of Information

The organisation, which works to improve public access to official information and to ensure the FOI Act is implemented effectively, has collated 500 examples of press stories which were published following requests using the new act.

Among those included are stories from the *The Journal* in Newcastle, which revealed that four nurses, doctors or other NHS hospital workers are attacked in the North East every day, and the *Cumberland News*, which reported that almost 3,000 pupils were excluded from secondary schools in Carlisle between 2000 and 2004.

The *Leicester Mercury* revealed how one Leicestershire dental practice is earning nearly £1m a year in fees for treating NHS patients, and the *Western Mail* told how the Ministry of Defence has investigated 28 reports of UFO sightings in Wales since 2002.

Other regional newspapers which feature in the report include the *Manchester Evening News, Coventry Evening Telegraph, Express and Star, Cambridge Evening News* and *Eastern Daily Press.*

Popular FOI requests included those relating to topics such as speed cameras, MRSA, parking fees, compensation claims and council expenses.

The FOI Act came into force on 1 January 2005, and the report includes disclosures under the UK and Scottish FOI Acts.

It is thought the 500 stories included are only a small sample of all FOI disclosures in the act's first year.

⇨ This article was published on 26 July 2006. Visit www.holdthefrontpage.co.uk for more information.

© *holdthefrontpage.co.uk*

Freedom of information

Everyone has the right to request information held by public sector organisations under the Freedom of Information Act 2000, which came into force in January 2005

The Freedom of Information (FOI) Act

The FOI gives you the right to ask any public body for all the information they have on any subject you choose. Also, unless there's a good reason, the organisation must provide the information within a month. You can also ask for all the personal information they hold on you.

Scotland has its own Freedom of Information Act, which is very similar to the England, Wales and Northern Ireland Act. If the public authority you want to make a request to operates only in Scotland then your request will be handled under the Scottish Act instead.

Public sector bodies covered by the Act

The Freedom of Information Act applies to all 'public authorities' including:
⇨ government departments and local assemblies;
⇨ local authorities and councils;
⇨ heath trusts, hospitals and doctors' surgeries;
⇨ schools, colleges and universities;
⇨ publicly funded museums;
⇨ the police;
⇨ lots of other non-departmental public bodies, committees and advisory bodies.

Who can access the information?

Any person can make a request for information under the Act – there are no restrictions on your age, nationality, or where you live.

What can you ask for?

You can ask for any information at all – but some information might be withheld to protect various interests which are allowed for by the Act. If this is case, the public authority must tell you why they have withheld information.

If you ask for information about yourself, then your request will be handled under the Data Protection Act instead of the Freedom of Information Act.

How to make a request

All you have to do is write to (or email) the public authority that you think holds the information you want. You should make sure that you include:
⇨ your name;
⇨ an address where you can be contacted;
⇨ a description of the information that you want.

You don't have to mention the Freedom of Information Act, but there is no reason not to if you want to. You should try to describe the information you want in as much detail as possible: for example, say 'minutes of the meeting where the decision to do X was made', rather than 'everything you have about X'. This will help the public authority find the information you need.

All public authorities must manage their information in accordance with a publication scheme which describes the 'classes' or 'kinds' of information held (such as minutes or reports). It is worth bearing this in mind when you make your request.

How long does it take?

Public authorities must comply with your request promptly, and should provide the information to you within 20 working days (around a month). If they need more time, they must write and tell you when they will answer, and why they need more time.

What does it cost?

Most requests are free. You might be asked to pay a small amount for making photocopies or postage.

If the public authority thinks that it will cost them more than £450 (or £600 for a request to central government) to find the information and prepare it for release, then they can turn down your request. They might ask you to narrow down your request by being more specific in the information you're looking for.

How you receive the information

When you make a request you may ask that the information be given to you in a particular form. However, a public authority may take into account the cost of supplying the information in this form before complying with your request.

You should be able to receive the information:
⇨ in permanent form;
⇨ in summary form;
⇨ or by permission to inspect records containing the information.

You may also be able to receive it:

⇨ in Braille;
⇨ in audio format;
⇨ in large type;
⇨ translated into another language.

Copyright and restrictions

The Freedom of Information Act does not place restrictions on how you may use the information you receive under it. However, the Act does not transfer copyright in any information supplied under it. If you plan to reproduce the information you receive, you should ensure that you will not be breaching anyone's copyright by doing so.

Your right of appeal

If your request for information is refused, you should first ask the public authority for an internal review of their decision. Someone in the authority who was not connected with the initial decision should carry out this review.

If you have already done this, or the public authority refuses to review their decision, you can appeal to the independent Information Commissioner. He has the power to investigate the way the public authority handled your request and the answer they gave. If he agrees that they have wrongly withheld information, he can order them to disclose it to you.

The Information Tribunal

If you disagree with the way the Information Commissioner responds to your appeal you may appeal against it. This will be handled by the Information Tribunal. This is strictly for use when you dispute the Information Commissioner's response and not the public authority or any other party's acts.

Requests for environmental information

In addition to the rights mentioned above, if you request information about the environment it cannot be refused just because of what it would cost the public authority to comply. This includes information about the air and atmosphere, water, soil, land, landscape, substances, energy, noise, radiation or waste, emissions, discharges and so on, as well as information about policies which affect these things.

⇨ This information is reprinted with permission from the Central Office of Information. Visit www.direct.gov.uk for more information.

© Crown copyright

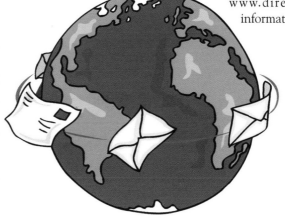

'Unacceptable' freedom of information delays

Information from the Campaign for Freedom of Information

The unacceptable delays experienced by many people using the Freedom of Information Act are highlighted in official statistics published today.

The Campaign for Freedom of Information said the government's figures showed that a 'disturbing' level of requests were not being dealt with within the Act's time limits. The figures show that:

⇨ more than a third of all requests to government departments (36%) took longer than the Act's 20 working-day deadline to answer.

⇨ although extensions are permitted for some types of requests, departments must tell applicants they need the extra time within 20 days of the request. Departments failed to meet this deadline in a quarter of all cases (25%).

⇨ The Home Office had the worst record of any government department. In 60% of all requests it failed either to respond to the request within 20 days, or even tell the applicant that it needed more time within that period. The Campaign said this represented routine disregard for the Act's requirements.

⇨ The Department of Health failed to tell applicants that it needed an extension within the required time in 43% of all its requests and the Department of Trade and Industry overshot the deadline in 33% of cases.

Other departments were substantially more successful: the Department for Transport and the Department for Constitutional Affairs both answered 83% of their requests within the basic 20 working-day period. The Department for Work and Pensions met this time limit in 81% of cases and the Ministry of Defence, which received far more requests than any other department, met the 20 day limit for 71% of its requests.

However, the Campaign was critical of the fact that the monitoring statistics failed to show how long people actually had to wait for replies. The Campaign's director Maurice Frankel said:

'The government is only measuring how long departments take to tell people that their requests will be delayed – without telling us anything about the actual delays. As long as you have been told within 20 days that your request is going to be delayed, the report says the department has dealt with it successfully. But the real test is how long you have to wait for an answer, whether this is 2, 3 or even 4 months – and the report is completely silent about this.'

The figures also showed substantial variation in the percentage of requests granted in full. The Department of Transport was top of the list, answering 76% of all requests in full, followed by the Ministry of Defence which provided full answers to 67% of all requests. The Campaign said that the actual FOI responses published by these departments on their websites showed that they were genuinely pushing forward the boundaries of disclosure. At the other end of the scale the Department of Trade and Industry provided full answers in only 21% of cases, the Home Office in 28% and the Cabinet Office in 29% of cases.

The Campaign said the report showed substantial variation between departments.

'Some departments may deal with more sensitive materials than others, but it's also clear that some parts of Whitehall are more committed to freedom of information than others,' it said.

Notes:

⇨ *Public authorities can take longer than 20 working days to respond to a request where the Act requires them to consider disclosing exempt information on public interest grounds. In this case they are allowed a 'reasonable' extension, but must tell the applicant that they need the extra time within 20 working days of receiving the request.*

⇨ *The statistics are published by the Department for Constitutional Affairs on its website. See: 'Freedom of Information Act 2000. Statistics on Implementation in Central Government. Q1. January–March 2005.'*

⇨ This information was released on 23 June 2005. It is reprinted with permission from the Campaign for Freedom of Information. Visit www.cfoi.org.uk for more information.

© *Campaign for Freedom of Information*

Two-year FOI battle over 'Donnygate' quiz ends in victory for the Star

The *Sheffield Star* has claimed victory in a two-year Freedom of Information battle with a local council.

Doncaster Council has been ordered to disclose details about excessive expense claims made by officers and councillors – after the Information Commissioner examined a rejected request for the information by the paper.

The newspaper approached the council for details about claims by officers and councillors dating back to the Donnygate saga during which the Audit Commissioner said council representatives had enjoyed a 'jet set lifestyle' at ratepayers' expense, leading to some people facing criminal prosecutions.

Many were ordered to pay back money they had overclaimed and others, who were not prosecuted, were asked to give back at least part of expenses claims which were considered to be excessive.

The *Star* made its original request within days of the new FOI Act coming into force in 2005, asking for the names of those who had since repaid money to the council, as well as details of the amounts each individual had repaid.

Doncaster Council refused outright and the newspaper approached the Information Commissioner to arbitrate.

After a two-year battle, the *Star* claimed a victory over the council when the commissioner ordered that at least some of the information sought should be made public.

Editor Alan Powell said the paper was delighted with the outcome of the application as it showed newspapers could overcome a culture of secrecy and obstruction.

He said: 'It is also encouraging that the Information Commissioner pulled no punches in criticising Doncaster Council for failing to assist us in the early stages of our application.

'This has been a long and, at times, frustrating chase for information which we believe the public has a right to know. This money was spent by their representatives supposedly on their behalf and it is unacceptable that someone should feel that the public should be kept in the dark over the details.

'One particularly infuriating aspect came when the council refused to disclose details of the repayments, claiming it would be an infringement of the Data Protection Act. We suspect that, as this case happened some years ago, some of those involved will be dead. How can the Act be applied to dead people?

'This is an area we will investigate further. Despite what Doncaster Council wishes, Donnygate is not dead.'

The council was also reprimanded for failing to fulfil its obligations under the Freedom of Information Act, which states that organisations have a duty to help a complainant narrow down their inquiry if it is felt to be too broad, which proved to be the case with that made by the *Star*.

In its ruling, the Information Commissioner said the council should reveal details of all repayments made as a result of criminal proceedings and that the authority should disclose the total amount repaid.

The council has 35 days either to respond to the application or to appeal.

⇨ This article was published on 31 January 2007. Visit www.holdthefrontpage.co.uk for more information.

Protection of sources upheld in High Court

Information from the National Union of Journalists

The National Union of Journalists is hailing today's High Court ruling that journalist Robin Ackroyd should not have to reveal his source as a historic victory, upholding the highest principles of the profession.

Robin Ackroyd, a freelance journalist who wrote an article about the treatment in hospital of Moors Murderer Ian Brady, won his right to protect his source after a six–year legal battle with the Mersey Care NHS Trust. His case was backed throughout by the NUJ and the union's lawyers Thompsons.

Mr Justice Tugendhat said that Robin was a 'responsible journalist whose purpose was to act in the public interest'. He confirmed that there is 'a vital public interest' in the protection of a journalist's sources.

In a statement issued straight afterwards Robin said: 'The way a society treats its prisoners, patients – indeed each and every citizen, including journalists – is a test of its maturity.

'Ian Brady, as odious as his crimes were, was mishandled and mistreated. This was and still is a matter of public interest, not least because it has led to the longest running hunger strike in British penal history.

'I investigated the facts and the issues and today my efforts have been vindicated – as they were when, seven years ago, a judicial inquiry urged the government to "grasp the nettle" and close Ashworth. The institution was described as "dysfunctional". Managers were secretive and out of touch. Reports were suppressed. Ministers, officials, the press – and thereby the public – were misled.'

Robin Ackroyd gave extracts from Brady's medical records to the *Daily Mirror*, which printed them in an article in December 1999.

The House of Lords ordered the *Daily Mirror* to disclose the source of the leaked medical records. When Robin came forward, the Ashworth secure hospital launched legal proceedings against him to reveal his source.

Today's High Court ruling confirms that someone trying to get a journalist to reveal their source must prove a 'pressing social need' for the source to be disclosed. After the Human Rights Act that includes a rigorous analysis of all the circumstances of the case. The court said that one of these is the public interest in protecting a journalist's sources.

'[The defendant] has a record of investigative journalism which has been authoritatively recognised, so that it would not be in the public interest that his sources should be discouraged from speaking to him where it is appropriate that they do so.'

NUJ General Secretary Jeremy Dear said: 'This is a fantastic result for Robin and for all journalists. The fundamental point of principle – that there is a strong public interest in upholding journalists' right not to reveal their sources – has been maintained.

'Robin has showed huge courage in standing true to this principle during six very difficult years. We all owe him an immense debt of gratitude – all journalists are in a stronger and safer position because of the brave stand he has taken.

'The NUJ supported Robin every step of the way and, thanks to the excellent work of our solicitors Thompsons, we have won the day. Justice has finally been done.'

Mersey Care NHS Trust have been given leave to appeal.

⇨ This article was published on 7 February 2006. It is reprinted with permission from the National Union of Journalists. Visit www.nuj.org.uk for more information.

Royal scoop too hot to handle

A pioneering citizen photojournalism start-up turned down the scoop of a lifetime when it declined to act as a sales agent for a private video of the Royal Family at home

Scoopt.com, a new agency which sells amateur-taken photographs to newspapers and magazines, decided that the invasion of privacy involved was too severe and the legal risks too great to justify using the video, which it returned to the person who offered it to the company.

'It involved the Royal Family, a video of the Royal Family. Essentially it was private pictures and videos of the Royal Family taken for a particular event that through some bizarre sequence of events ended up with somebody who sent it to us,' Kyle MacRae, the founder of Scoopt, told OUT-LAW Radio, the weekly technology law podcast.

'My initial instinct was that this is private. We then considered it commercially and thought actually this could be pretty valuable,' he said. 'But you have got all sorts of issues involved. We don't own the copyright nor do we have any legitimate licence to that copyright, nor does the Scoopt member who sent it to us. Do we have an overriding public interest story? Is it worth it? Is this going to change the nature of the Monarchy in Britain?

'If any of that is true then, yes, we put it out to market, if it shows some kind of blatant hypocrisy on the part of the Royal Family then great, we've got a news story. In this case it was just completely harmless, it was innocuous, it was nice,' said MacRae. 'We weighed all that up and 24 hours later we just decided we weren't going to handle this.'

Scoopt was established 18 months ago in order to represent people who used cameras and phones to capture important news events or celebrity gaffes. As cheap digital cameras and camera phones have spread, so has so-called 'citizen media', where ordinary people provide the pictures and videos used by mainstream outlets, often for significant fees.

'We're the broker between members of the public and mainstream media,' MacRae said. 'So if somebody happens to get a newsworthy photograph or video and they want to make some money out of that it's very, very hard for the man in the street to deal directly with the press, so they come through us and we then license that content commercially, at professional prices.'

Copyright stays with the creator of the content, while Scoopt and that person split revenue 50/50, said MacRae.

The agency supplied the pictures of US baseball star Cory Liddle's plane, which he crashed into the side of a skyscraper in New York last year. Scoopt-brokered images were carried on the front page of *The Times* and *The Guardian*, as well as by *The Sun* and other papers internationally.

MacRae says that his agency tries to operate ethically, which is why it turned down the Royal video, and why it advises would-be snappers to behave in a humane manner.

'We've been asked in an accusatory tone sometimes that by waving the dollar signs at people are we encouraging people to become paparazzi. Or, more seriously, to put themselves in danger,' said MacRae. 'I think there is a risk that people will go too far. If you come across an event where people need help then help them, don't take photos.'

'A professional photo-journalist can probably justify shooting rather than helping, that's their job. Members of the public aren't, it's just the wrong thing to do, you drop the camera, you help where you possibly can then you get yourself the hell out into a position of safety,' said MacRae.

⇨ This information is reprinted with permission from Pinsent Masons. Visit www.out-law.com for more information.

Reuters reacts to doctored photos

Reuters has removed 920 photographs from its database following reports that a Lebanese freelancer had doctored images of the conflict between Israel and Lebanese group Hizbollah

The agency reported that software was used to make the damage inflicted by an Israeli air strike on Beirut look worse than it was in an image that appeared on news websites on Saturday.

Reuters said the photograph was taken and doctored by freelancer Adnan Hajj using Adobe Photoshop software. The practice is sometimes known as 'Photoshopping'.

The picture's accuracy was first questioned in a posting to a blog called Little Green Footballs. A Reuters photographer in Canada read the posting and alerted his editors. Reuters quickly terminated its relationship with Hajj and began investigating all his work. A second doctored image was found: a photo of an Israeli F-16 warplane in action over Lebanon that ran on 2nd August, amended to increase the number of flares dropped by the plane.

On Monday, Reuters posted a statement in its online picture archive saying that, as a precautionary measure, it has withdrawn all photos taken by Hajj. It added: 'Reuters has tightened its editing procedure for photographs of the conflict and regrets any inconvenience caused.'

'There is no graver breach of Reuters standards for our photographers than the deliberate manipulation of an image,' said Global Picture Editor Tom Szlukovenyi. 'Reuters has zero tolerance for any doctoring of pictures and constantly reminds its photographers, both staff and freelance, of this strict and unalterable policy.'

In 2003, the *LA Times* sacked a photographer in similar circumstances. Brian Walski was accused of digitally altering an image of a British soldier directing Iraqi civilians to take cover from Iraqi fire on the outskirts of Basra to make it look more dramatic.

The *LA Times* and Reuters' strict policies against doctoring are reflected in the UK Press Complaints Commission's Code of Practice:

> ## 'There is no graver breach of Reuters standards for our photographers than the deliberate manipulation of an image'

'The Press must take care not to publish inaccurate, misleading or distorted information, including pictures,' it says.

It adds: 'A significant inaccuracy, misleading statement or distortion once recognised must be corrected, promptly and with due prominence, and – where appropriate – an apology published.'

⇨ This article was published on 10 August 2006. It is reprinted with permission from Pinsent Masons. Visit www.out–law.com for more information.

© *Pinsent Masons*

"Hmm... not dramatic enough. Needs more smoke and tears."

A snap too far

Will the press be responsible for the introduction of a new privacy law?
Lyra McKee thinks so

'All of us are responsible for this fascination with the sordid goings-on in the lives of the rich and famous.'

Yes! They've finally done it! The scandal-thirsty media in Hong Kong or to be more specific the 'paps' have nailed their own coffin well and truly shut. Our snap-happy friends have finally overstepped the fine line between doing their job and stalking celebrities for gratuitous titillation.

This time their telephoto lenses were focused on the young songstress, Gillian Chung, as she adjusted her bra backstage during a concert. No doubt there will be a rise in sales of Agent Provocateur lingerie in China.

If only that was the sole consequence of their foolish behaviour it wouldn't matter at all. The actor Jackie Chan and other celebs marched to Hong Kong's government headquarters to hand over a petition urging the politicians to tighten the laws regarding 'lads' mags' and 'gossip rags'. Needless to say the local hacks are fuming and screaming censorship!

Inevitably the introduction of these laws will mean a return to some degree of press censorship. The ill-judged actions of a few could result in the punishment of the many. It would be foolish to think that it couldn't happen here.

If the British and European paparazzi and tabloid editors don't toe the line or practise some sort of self-censorship these laws will soon be introduced in our country. And who's to say that it will stop there? Tony Blair and his like will have the media by the scruff of the neck over every little bit of gossip they write about, or for every photo they take. And maybe he'd be right too.

If the Chinese government bows to the pressure – and let's face it, they've done so in the past – then journalists, photographers and every other media practitioner will suffer. Needless to say so, also, will the truth.

All of us are responsible for this fascination with the sordid goings-on in the lives of the rich and famous. If we didn't want to read about it and see the pictures there would be no-one to write about it or take the photos. You get the media you deserve, I suppose. I know I have had that fascination and I really shouldn't.

If things carry on as they are then governments will act and the media will pay for their past indiscretions. Strangely enough, this was a moment foreseen by many people, an accident, we all knew, that was waiting to happen.

There is little point in journalists complaining and shouting about censorship now. It's too late. The damage has already been done. Where were these journalists when the stars complained before about media intrusion? They should have listened earlier and got their house in order. Today it is Hong Kong, tomorrow it will be the world. Journalists, paparazzi and editors the world over will have nobody to blame for future censorship but themselves.

⇨ This information is repri̱ ̱ ̱d
with permission from Hea̱ ̱ers.
Visit www.headliners.oṟ more
information. ̱ 06 Headliners

Media responsibility and personal privacy

Information from Channel 4 Learning

Most people enjoy reading stories about famous people and their lives. Certain celebrities' pictures on the front cover of a newspaper or magazine can hugely increase sales, so media companies know that's what we must be interested in. A film star on holiday, a pop singer falling out of a nightclub drunk, a married celebrity spotted snogging someone they shouldn't be. It's all good fun. They're famous after all and should expect it. That's what a free press is all about.

In their shoes

What if it was you? What if you'd won the lottery? Great! The newspapers want a picture and an interview – wow! Fame for 15 minutes! But what if they then started following you around. They want to see what you're spending your money on, where you're going, how your life has changed.

They start finding your friends and family and asking them questions. Stories begin to get printed about your past. You open your front door in the morning to a crowd of photographers on your doorstep. How might you feel then? All good fun? Probably not. You would probably feel hassled and as if you have no privacy whatsoever.

Press protection

The 'Press Code' sets down guidelines for the media to ensure that they are acting responsibly and not invading people's privacy. This is produced by the Press Complaints Commission, which is responsible for investigating any complaints about what has been printed in the papers or magazines.

The Commission investigates thousands of complaints every year. If the press breaks the code there's not much the Press Complaints Commission can do – the damage has already been done. However, if the press goes too far, there are laws to put things right.

What does the Press Code say?

Among other things, it states that anything published has to be accurate and should never mislead people by using pictures that have been changed or distorted. Individuals' private and family lives have to be respected. Journalists mustn't pester people for stories and information. They shouldn't intrude on children while they are at school and they mustn't be prejudiced. Do you think newspapers do this? Which type of newspaper do you think is more likely to break the code?

The law

If the media release a story with completely incorrect facts, then the people or person it was about can take the company to court for libel or slander. Slander is when things have been said about someone that aren't true, for example in a TV report. Libel is when untrue things are printed in a newspaper or magazine. This is against the law and some newspapers and magazines regularly find themselves in court... ...ble.

Big questions

⇨ Do you think that famous people have a right to complete privacy?
⇨ We buy more newspapers and magazines with stories about famous people than newspapers with serious news in them. Is it ha?se of us that celebrities get ...
⇨ If we... the press?
   do you th?have a press how the governm? would affect

Key points

⇨ The media have a responsibility to let us know what's going on.
⇨ The Press Code is a set of guidelines that journalists should follow to ensure that people's privacy is kept and that reports are accurate.
⇨ If a newspaper or magazine prints something that's incorrect, complaints can be made to the Press Complaints Commission.
⇨ There are laws to protect individuals against libel and slander.

Reality bytes: Stan Collymore

Footballers always seem to make it into the news and not always for the right reasons. Stan Collymore, a footballer, appeared on the front page of *The Sun* with the headline 'I lied'. The front page claimed that he had lied about being beaten up in a Dublin bar by some rugby players.

The paper claimed that the rugby players had signed a confession to prove it. It had actually been a stunt by the newspaper and the confession had been signed by getting someone to pretend they were a fan asking for an autograph. Although on the inside of the paper it did say it was a stunt, this wasn't made clear on the front page that people were more likely to look at.

Stan Collymore made a complaint to the Press Complaints Commission that this was against the Press Code. The Commission agreed and apologies had to be made. Do you think being a celebrity is a help or a hindrance in such cases?

⇨ This information is reprinted with permission from the Channel 4 Learning website. Visit www.channel4learning.net for more information.

© Expresso Broadband Limited

Journalists given new freedom under libel law

By Simon Moore

Journalists have won the freedom to publish news articles that contain allegations about public figures without the threat from libel.

As long as their reporting is in the public interest, and has been undertaken in a seriously responsible manner, then it can be published without repercussions under English law.

Such is the verdict of the House of Lords, which yesterday found that even if newsworthy allegations later emerge as defamatory and false, journalists can publish without fear of reprisals.

Handed down yesterday, the ruling is a green-light to journalists, editors and their publications to more rigorously pursue newsworthy persons, free from the 'chilling' effect of lawsuits.

For journalists, the move also strengthens the so-called 'Reynolds privilege' established in 2001, which implies a defence against libel on the grounds the public interest was being served.

The Lords were concerned with an article published in 2002 by the *Wall Street Journal*, 'an unsensational newspaper,' they said, which stated that Saudi officials were cooperating with the US government in monitoring bank accounts.

The 2 February article, entitled *Saudi officials monitor certain bank accounts*, was found to have defamed a Saudi businessman and a company belonging to his business group, of which he is president, two courts found.

But the Lords dismissed these verdicts, disagreeing with both the High Court and the Appeal Court, which stated the WSJ should pay £40,000 to the defamed businessman, Mohammed Jameel.

They said the 'thrust' of the WSJ's article was to inform the public that the two nations were in contact, as

the US Treasury had demanded that the Kingdom's central bank reveal if the accounts of prominent Saudis were siphoning money to terrorists.

This was 'succinctly stated in the first paragraph,' the Lords said.

'This [story] was, without doubt, a matter of high international importance, a very appropriate matter for report by a serious newspaper,' they added, pointing out that although an ally to the US, Saudi Arabia's status was then precarious, compounded by the 9/11 hijackers being of Saudi origin.

They added: 'But it was a difficult matter to investigate and report since information was not freely available in the Kingdom and the Saudi authorities.'

It was also difficult to verify the allegations, which journalists are bound to do under libel law, because the existence of covert surveillance by the highly secretive Saudi authorities would be impossible to prove by evidence in open court.

Delivering his ruling, Lord Hoffman hinted that it was practically impossible for the journalist and second journalist of the WSJ article to meet their commitments of verification as media professionals, however attempts were made.

Lord Hoffman's report to the House of Lords, England's highest court, says a 'more detailed consideration' should have been given to the Reynolds privilege by both the High Court and Appeal Court judges.

It's a view shared by Alistair Brett, legal manager of Times Newspapers.

'Most media lawyers would agree and point the finger at the two judges in charge of libel actions, Mr Justice

Eady and Mr Justice Gray. Both came in for criticism in Jameel on how they have applied the old law in what should be a new context and effectively denied the press the benefit of the Reynolds public interest defence over the past six years,' he wrote on *Times Online*, the paper's website.

'From now on, the House of Lords will have breathed new life into responsible investigative journalism. The judgment is as refreshing as it is overdue.'

Freelance journalists should note that in legal scrutiny of editorial decisions, 'weight should ordinarily be given to the professional judgment of an editor or journalist in the absence of some indication that it was made in a casual, cavalier, slipshod or careless manner'.

Despite the green-light for journalists to enjoy greater freedom, on the grounds they report responsibly and in the public interest, freelancers should note; there remains no protection for so-called 'kiss-and-tell' stories.

'The public interest comes out on top. But that expression has its own particular meaning – just because something may engage the interest of the public does not necessarily make it in the public interest – so this judgment will not be carte blanche for the gossip press,' Roger Sinclair, media lawyer at Egos Ltd, said in an interview with Freelance UK.

'Secondly, there is a clear duty on the journalist and publisher to take reasonable steps to be sure that what is published is accurate and fit for publication – it has been said that no public interest is served by publishing or communicating misinformation.'

⇨ This article first appeared on Freelance UK on 13 October 2006. Visit www.freelanceuk.com for more information.

Teenage magazines, a responsible medium

Information from the Teenage Magazine Arbitration Panel

Teenage magazines are the most responsible medium teenagers can access, according to Celia Duncan, editor of *Cosmogirl*, addressing delegates at the Teenage Magazine Arbitration Panel (TMAP) annual forum.

Duncan told delegates that the teenage magazine sector was 'the most regulated' in the marketplace and that editors followed the TMAP guidelines 'incredibly closely.' Despite this the *Cosmogirl* editor cricised the 'hysteria and paranoia to protect teenagers all the time'. Duncan pointed to food advertising guidelines threatening advertising revenues and periodic critical headlines in newspapers as two examples of how the sector was unfairly undermined.

Speaking at the event on Monday 20 November, Duncan was joined on an editors' panel also comprising: Alison Begbie, acting editor of *Bliss* magazine; Diane Leeming, features director, *Sugar*; Leslie Sinoway, editor of *Mizz* magazine and Rosalie Snaith, editor of *It's Hot!*

The panel discussed the impact of technology on teenage magazine brands, how magazines can help combat social problems for young people including bullying and underage drinking and the important role they play promoting sexual health awareness. According to TMAP chair Fleur Fisher:

'We (teenage magazines) are recognised by Government as being experts at communicating with people, not talking at them.'

Teenagers from Thomas Tallis school took part in a discussion on making online safer for younger people. According to Fisher the key was finding a balance between their rights to access information with staying safe in 'the internet age'. She described parents in today's age as 'technology migrants' compared to their 'technology native' children.

The role of teenage magazines in the sexual health of young people

In 1996 Peter Luff, Tory MP for Worcester, proposed a Bill which would require publishers to place age suitability warnings on the cover of young women's magazines, in an effort to allay concerns about their use of sexually explicit material.

This report examines the debate on teenage magazines and analyses the current sources of information available to young people on sexual-related issues. As a review of current research, this document suggests that there is certainly an important role for teenage magazines in the sexual health education of young people, and that they provide information which can empower young people to make informed choices on sexual issues.

A key factor in this debate is the emergence of more open discussion about sex, following the increasing concern about AIDS. A new explicit language has become necessary and therefore more acceptable to society. In this context, is it realistic to accuse teenage magazines of creating this new sexually aware teenage girl or are teenage magazines merely reflecting the way this age group is changing within society? More specifically is criticism of these magazines a case of shooting the messenger?

This research clearly indicates that young people prefer to get their information on sex from printed sources rather than from adults and that there is a need to ensure that teenage magazines continue to contain information which enable young people to adopt safer sex behaviour and exercise healthy choices in their personal lives.

⇨All information on this page is reprinted with permission from the Teenage Magazine Arbitration Panel. Visit www.tmap.org.uk for more information, including a copy of the report referred to in this article.

© *Teenage Magazine Arbitration Panel*

Do lads' mags teach young men about sex and relationships?

Why Ofsted's report on personal, social and health education is wide of the mark, by Dr Petra Boynton

Today's newspapers have all been eagerly covering a report from Ofsted (the UK's official school inspection body) that reviews personal, social and health education (PHSE).

Although the report covers a number of issues, the media focus has mostly been around criticising parents for not talking about sex and praising magazines for offering sex advice:

'Parents' health advice under fire from schools watchdog' – *The Guardian*

'Pupils rely on magazines to learn about sex' – *The Scotsman*

'Ofsted praises teen mags for teaching sex' – *Telegraph*

'Magazines, not parents, teach the facts of life' – *Daily Mail*

In particular the press picked up on lads' magazines offering sex information, and the media coverage would have you believe the main focus of the Ofsted report is about media sex education. However, a reading of the 26-page report suggests otherwise, with only two sections tackling media:

'In discussion, pupils report that some of their parents have neither the knowledge nor skill to talk to them directly about sensitive issues. Parents often seek to approach personal, social and health issues with their children tangentially, if at all. As well as failing to provide the information themselves, some parents express concern about the suitability of information that young people receive from other sources, such as magazines, even when these could be useful. For example, the increase in the number of magazines aimed at young men, while at times reinforcing sexist attitudes, has helped to redress the balance of advice available to young people.'

The range of topics and the explicitness in dealing with them have increased in many of the magazines read by young people. While many magazines now stress the importance of safe sex, some communicate, inaccurately, the perception that all young people are sexually active. Nevertheless, the "problem pages" in magazines remain a very positive source of advice and reassurance for many young people, but difficulties may arise if the messages clash with parental and cultural norms.'

It isn't clear why this angle got so much coverage, since the Ofsted press release didn't focus on this issue. However, it seems one of the newswires did spin the story towards the 'magazines as main source of sex education' angle which many papers uncritically ran with. It's pretty obvious that very few of them bothered to read the full report – even though it's not all that long and is easily available online.

Whilst it is positive that problem pages are praised, it is important to recognise – which Ofsted did not – that the standard of advice giving varies widely across print and online publications. Some have qualified, vetted staff writing for them while others are written by unqualified staffers, 'sexperts' or celebrities. This means some magazines offer quality information, others are very misleading.

What is worrying about the Ofsted report is the assumption that because lads' magazines exist they automatically offer an opportunity for advice giving to young men. Evidence and experience of sex educators working in the media suggests this is completely untrue. Having lads' magazines available has done little to increase young men's knowledge of sexual health issues – but has led to an increase in incorrect sex information being given – in particular encouraging sexually coercive behaviour.

⇨ This article was published on 12 April 2007. Reprinted with permission from Dr Petra Boynton. Visit www.drpetra.co.uk for more information.

© *Dr Petra Boynton*

Suicide coverage: time to take stock

By Professor Mike Jempson from MediaWise

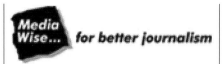
for better journalism

When people kill themselves we are all shocked. When newspapers are given the go–ahead to publish pictures of a suicide it is equally shocking.

The Press Complaints Commission (PCC) has justified publication, by the *London Evening Standard*, *The Sun* and *The Times*, of a picture of a woman leaping to her death. Most newspapers decided against using the pictures.

In a hand-wringing adjudication the PCC explains that it cannot make judgements about 'taste and decency', yet it acknowledges that the *Evening Standard* merely assumed that the family had been informed before publishing a photograph of Katherine Ward's death. One of the first rules of journalism is 'never assume anything: always check your facts'.

The Samaritans, whose guidelines were breached by the three newspapers, have expressed their disappointment at the adjudication. MediaWise regards it as yet another example of the PCC's effrontery as a 'self-regulator'. Under the guidelines we devised with the National Union of Journalists Ethics Council the photographs would not have appeared.

We have regularly reminded the PCC over many years about the sensitivities of suicide reporting, the risk of copycat behaviour, and the need for a special Clause in the Editors' Code of Practice to highlight the need for care when reporting newsworthy suicides.

We have supplied the PCC with copies of Kathryn Williams and Keith Hawton's 2001 study, 'Suicidal Behaviour and the Media: Findings from a systematic review of research literature,' which clearly illustrates the link between coverage and suicidal behaviour from evidence around the world.

The guidelines we produced in 2003 with the NUJ Ethics Council have been welcomed by UK editors and are in use internationally. This is not a matter of taste and decency, but of life and death. All the evidence suggests that sensitive reporting can save lives.

Note:
In 2006 the Editors' Code of Practice added a sub-clause, 'When reporting suicide, care should be taken to avid excessive detail about the method used'.

⇨ This information was released on 4 April 2004. It is reprinted with permission from MediaWise. Visit www.mediawise.org.uk for more information.

© *MediaWise*

Complaints to the Press Complaints Commission

Possible breaches of the Code – by clause

Clause 1	Accuracy	72.6%
Clause 2	Opportunity to reply	0.9%
Clause 3	Privacy	10.8%
Clause 4	Harassment	4.3%
Clause 5	Intrusion into grief or shock	4.7%
Clause 6	Children	2.1%
Clause 7	Children in sex cases	0%
Clause 8	Hospitals	0.6%
Clause 9	Reporting of crime	0%
Clause 10	Clandestine devices and subterfuge	0.5%
Clause 11	Victims of sexual assault	0.1%
Clause 12	Discrimination	2.6%
Clause 13	Financial journalism	0.1%
Clause 14	Confidential sources	0.5%
Clause 15	Witness payments in criminal trials	0.1%
Clause 16	Payment to criminals	0.1%

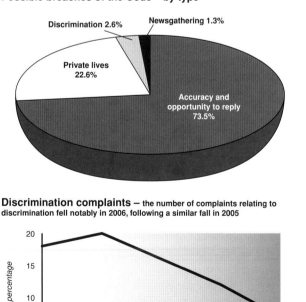

Possible breaches of the Code – by type

Discrimination 2.6%
Newsgathering 1.3%
Private lives 22.6%
Accuracy and opportunity to reply 73.5%

Discrimination complaints – the number of complaints relating to discrimination fell notably in 2006, following a similar fall in 2005

Source: Taken from the Press Complaints Commision's Annual Review 2006.

New news, future news

Information from Ofcom

Attitudes to news: engagement and disengagement with news

Almost everyone agreed that it's important to keep up to date with the news (90 per cent) but one-third (32 per cent) claimed only to follow the news when something important or interesting is happening.

There are indications of greater levels of disconnection to the content of news. Some 55 per cent of people agreed that much of the news on TV was not relevant to them, up from 34 per cent in 2002. Indicatively, more people in 2006 than 2002 agreed that they only followed the news when something important or interesting was happening (26 per cent compared to 32 per cent).

Some 22 per cent of the overall population can be classified as news absorbed (defined as using three or more platforms for news, and agreeing strongly with the statements 'it's important to keep up to date with news and current affairs' and 'I like to use a variety of news sources so I can compare how they report stories'), and 13 per cent as news detached.

Those aged 16–19 are least likely to be news absorbed, although those aged 20–24 and 25–44 show little difference between them, suggesting that the belief of younger people that they will 'grow into' news as they get older is a correct one. That said, it is of note that those aged 45–64 are more likely to be news absorbed, and less likely to be detached.

Socio-economic group is also a factor in the extent to which people are news absorbed.

Nearly one-third of those in socio-economic group AB (29 per cent) can be classified this way, compared to 19 per cent of those in the DE group. Only 7 per cent of ABs can be classified as news detached, compared to nearly one in five (19 per cent) of DEs.

While news helps just under half (43 per cent) feel part of the democratic process, almost as many (37 per cent) claimed that TV news puts them off politics.

One-third of people over 20 can be said to be politically/socially engaged (defined through taking into account voting behaviour and involvement in politics, local community issues or campaigns). They are more likely to be interested in 'serious' news topics.

Overall, their 'appetite' for news is greater than the overall population, and they are more likely to have concerns about news ownership and sponsorship.

This segment of the population is more likely to use newspapers and radio for their news consumption than the rest of the population. However, crucially, they are no more likely to use the internet for news than the politically disengaged. Younger people who are politically engaged are more likely than the younger disengaged to use the internet for news.

While 16 per cent of 20–24s fall into the politically/socially engaged group, this rises to 40 per cent of those aged 45–65. Conversely, some 39 per cent of 20–24s are in the politically/socially disengaged segment, falling to 12 per cent of 45–64s.

Qualitative research particularly focused on disengagement with the young and minority ethnic groups and this elicited often very strong views

on the UK media. It explored various reasons for disengagement with the media, including:

⇨ Apathy – Particularly evident in the young. A feeling that they did not need to know what was covered in the news given conflicting priorities faced.

⇨ Cynicism – Reservations about the editorial policies and controls behind story selection and presentation.

⇨ Lack of relevance – Low interest in news content that people felt had little or no impact on them.

⇨ Disillusionment and distrust – Particularly amongst the minority ethnic groups arising from the perception that issues relating to their culture, race or faith were not treated fairly.

⇨ Other cultural affiliation – Consuming alternative media relating to non-UK cultures or particular faiths meant less opportunity to consume mainstream UK media (particularly for those in extended, multi-generational households).

News and young people

The 16–24 year-olds generally claimed less interest in news topics than their older counterparts. In particular, they were less interested in topics of a local or regional nature, current events, politics or business news than the older age groups. They were more interested in entertainment and celebrity news than older age groups.

Since 2002 there have been particular increases in young people claiming that they only watch news when something important or interesting is happening (33 per cent to 50 per cent) and that much of the news on TV is 'not relevant to me' has particularly increased (44 per cent to 64 per cent) – although this latter increase is similar to that for the UK population as a whole (34 per cent to 55 per cent).

The qualitative research found that many young people were cynical about news coverage and the levels of bias and exaggeration in the media. They distanced themselves from current events, politics and world affairs.

However, they tended to see this as being characteristic of their stage of life, and believed they would become more engaged as they got older and had more responsibilities. Some 81 per cent still say they think it's important to keep up with news and current affairs.

It is of note that young people were perceived not to appear onscreen enough in TV news programmes. While it is unsurprising that higher proportions of young people thought there were too few young people featured in news (53 per cent of 16–24 year-olds), around 45 per cent of 35–54 year-olds also thought the same.

News and people from minority ethnic groups

Respondents from minority ethnic groups were less likely to be interested in news – white respondents said they were interested in an average of 5.6 types of news, while people from minority ethnic groups were interested in an average of 4.1. Overall, there was less appetite for news across a variety

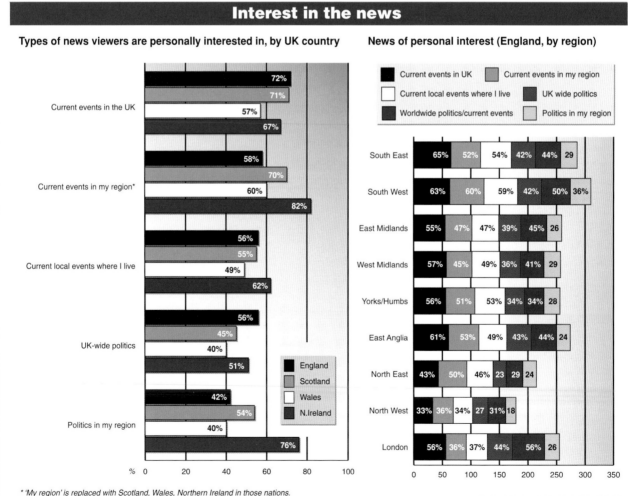

Interest in the news

Types of news viewers are personally interested in, by UK country

Current events in the UK: 72%, 71%, 57%, 67%
Current events in my region*: 58%, 70%, 60%, 82%
Current local events where I live: 56%, 55%, 49%, 62%
UK-wide politics: 56%, 45%, 40%, 51%
Politics in my region: 42%, 54%, 40%, 76%

England / Scotland / Wales / N.Ireland

% 0 20 40 60 80 100

* 'My region' is replaced with Scotland, Wales, Northern Ireland in those nations.

News of personal interest (England, by region)

Current events in UK | Current events in my region
Current local events where I live | UK wide politics
Worldwide politics/current events | Politics in my region

Region	Current events in UK	Current events in my region	Current local events where I live	UK wide politics	Worldwide politics/current events	Politics in my region
South East	65%	52%	54%	42%	44%	29
South West	63%	60%	59%	42%	50%	36
East Midlands	55%	47%	47%	39%	45%	26
West Midlands	57%	45%	49%	36%	41%	29
Yorks/Humbs	56%	51%	53%	34%	34%	28
East Anglia	61%	53%	49%	43%	44%	24
North East	43%	50%	46%	23	29	24
North West	33%	36%	34%	27	31%	18
London	56%	36%	37%	44%	56%	26

0 50 100 150 200 250 300 350

Source: New News, Future News, *Ofcom.*

of questions.

Some 46 per cent of people from minority ethnic groups felt that ethnic minorities get too little airtime compared to half as many (23 per cent) white respondents. This point was particularly driven by Black respondents: while 25 per cent of Asian respondents felt that this was the case, the corresponding figures for Black Caribbean and Black African respondents were much higher at 60 per cent and 61 per cent respectively.

People within specific ethnic groups had very different relationships with news. For example Black Africans were particularly interested in world-wide politics and current events – at 54 per cent this level of interest is significantly higher than that expressed by white and Asian respondents (both 41 per cent) and Black Caribbean respondents (36 per cent). Black Africans were also more likely to be interested in local/regional news than other minority groups. Asians were more likely to use the internet for news (36 per cent), whereas Black respondents were not particularly likely to use this platform (19 per cent).

Minority ethnic groups also differ in terms of their news absorption or detachment. One-quarter of Asians (25 per cent) can be classified as news absorbed, compared to 16 per cent of Black Africans and Caribbeans. Conversely, Asians are also more likely to be news detached – some 23 per cent can be classified in this way compared to 15 per cent of Black Africans and Caribbeans.

Qualitative research identified a strong feeling of dissatisfaction with the mainstream media in the UK. There was a common belief that the different UK media sources had their own agendas and particular stances and tones of reporting, although bias was seen as different for each group:

⇨ Black Caribbeans and Black Africans – annoyance that reporting over-emphasised links with criminal activity and produced a negative tone.

⇨ Muslims – dissatisfaction with coverage of terrorism and the Islamic faith.

⇨ Indian Hindus and Sikhs – more

satisfied with reporting of news relating to their communities, however there were objections to being classified as 'Asians' which they felt associated them with the negative portrayal of Muslims.

⇨ Those living in multi-generation households, where the elder generation had control of the main TV/radio, indicated in qualitative research that they often had less control over the news they consumed and so tended to be exposed to more news from, and related to, their culture, homeland or faith and therefore less UK news coverage.

Consumption: which news sources do people use?

Terrestrial television news remains ubiquitous as a news source – 94 per cent of people say they use it at some time, similar to the 91 per cent in 2002.

Reported use of the internet for news has doubled, from 15 per cent to 27 per cent. Highest internet use comes from the 25–44 age group (39 per cent). Use of the press and radio also show indicative changes since 2002.

Some 73 per cent of people claimed ever to use newspapers in 2006, compared to 67 per cent in 2002, and indications are that frequency of consumption has also decreased since 2002 – claimed daily use has gone from 43 per cent to 36 per cent. Similarly, use of the radio for news appears to have decreased overall (59 per cent to 52 per cent) and has also decreased in terms of claimed daily use (from 44 per cent to 35 per cent).

Consumption by the 16–24 age group appears to have decreased, particularly for newspapers (78 per cent to 61 per cent) and radio (60 per cent to 44 per cent).

English-language 24-hour TV channels are ever used by 36 per cent of the population, and foreign-language news channels by 4 per cent, which rises to 19 per cent of minority ethnic groups. Asians are more likely to use these (31 per cent) than either Black Africans or Black Caribbeans (6 per cent), reflecting the availability of particular channels.

Three-quarters of internet news consumption is through straightforward reading of news stories online, with one in five watching clips or personalised news services. TV channel news websites are nominated as used most, with online-only news aggregators next.

Blogs are rarely used (5 per cent of those who use the internet as a news source).

Use of mobile devices for news is low at 4 per cent, although this is strongly differentiated by age – 7 per cent of 16–24s use them compared to 1 per cent of those aged over 45.

People from minority ethnic groups are less likely to use most platforms for news than white respondents, with the exception of 24–hour news channels, the internet, and magazines. Asians are more likely to use the internet for news than Black Africans and Caribbeans, despite similar levels of penetration. People from minority ethnic groups use fewer sources of news overall.

Attitudes to news: opinions about TV news coverage

News coverage on the PSB (Public Service Broadcast) channels is seen as important by around three-quarters of the population, and the vast majority of people who watch particular news programmes on the PSB channels rate the particular programmes they saw as being high quality (91 per cent).

In terms of who is portrayed, however, celebrities are widely seen as getting too much airtime, and this concern has risen slightly since 2002 (65 per cent to 72 per cent).

Levels of concern over airtime for politicians are next highest, although these have barely changed since 2002 (60 per cent to 57 per cent).

People would like to see more ordinary people portrayed in the news. 'People like me' (46 per cent), ordinary people (45 per cent) and young people (40 per cent) were seen to get too little airtime.

⇨   This information is reprinted with permission from Ofcom. Visit www.ofcom.org.uk for more information.

© *Ofcom*

Cross-cultural analysis of the Danish Prophet Muhammad cartoons

Lessons to learn from the cultural clash between Denmark and Muslim, by Sahar El–Nadi, Culture Consultant, Cairo, Egypt

In September 2005, when a local Danish newspaper published some cartoons depicting Islam's Prophet Muhammad, they probably never expected the powerful adverse reaction it would evoke from millions of Muslims worldwide. At this time, there are probably many people around the world who are wondering what this is all about and want to know more about Muhammad, the man over whom this confrontation has erupted. Some would argue that this is a clash of civilisations, but to me, it looks more like a severe case of cross-cultural misunderstanding. This is an attempt at analysing the situation and extracting its valuable lessons.

The Quran declares to every human: 'O Mankind, We created you from a single (pair) of a male and a female and made you into nations and tribes, that you may know each other' 49:13.

It is probably the not 'knowing each other' that is at the core of the problem between Denmark and the Muslim nations.

How could difference in culture result in international confrontation?

Culture can be defined as a code of values, beliefs and traditions practised by a group of people, affecting their ideas and feelings. Culture is like a window through which people perceive the world outside.

Regarding the Danish cartoons, what seems to be the problem?

From the Muslim point of view, actually there are two problems rolled into one:

1. Drawing God or His Prophets is a taboo in Muslim culture, regardless of the nature of the drawing.

2. Mocking or tarnishing a Muslim holy symbol is absolutely unacceptable for Muslims: the cartoons portrayed Muhammad as an icon of violence, and Islam as a violent religion when in fact it is not.

What caused this cross-cultural clash?

Islam is conservative culture with defined limits. Muslims live their religion day-to-day, whereas modern western culture has loosened its grip on religious values as a way of life and substituted them for secularism instead, seeing prophets as odd historical figures, unfit for modern life. Therefore, it expects Muslims to be good secularists when it comes to free speech, while even secular Muslims object to insulting images of the Prophet; they in turn expect westerners to join them in their reverence for religious values.

Many basics of cross-cultural communication were missing in this situation:

Good cross-cultural communication requires many skills: speaking, listening, patience, flexibility, and basic knowledge of the unique identity and taboos of each side. It seems that both sides had exercised these skills very poorly in this situation:

Very few on either side speak the other's language; consequently true cultural communication was lost, as it was always through indirect channels.

In a cross-cultural setting with language barriers, it is important to avoid humour as it could undermine communication. In Denmark, cartoons are a common form of unrestricted expression, while in the Muslim world certain things cannot be the subject of jokes.

Different cultures may have different definitions for the same value: for example, while freedom of expression in Denmark may refer to unrestricted self-expression, the same value for Muslims does not allow transgressing anyone's holy symbols. Clash occurred when each side tenaciously held on to its own interpretation of the universal value of 'freedom of expression'. Cross-cultural disputes result from neglecting other's point of view, and trying to impose our ideas and beliefs on them.

Allowing heated emotions to block rational communication: the Muslims were offended that their respected prophet was mocked. In response, some chose to boycott Danish products, while others burned the Danish flag – which is a sacred symbol of national pride to the Danes. Suddenly, emotions rather than rational thinking steered the communication process into a dead end for cross-cultural understanding. It's destructive to communication to invalidate another human's personal feelings and thoughts, when that takes on a national perspective, we can only expect a heated confrontation.

Varying social values on each side: for example, emotional attachment to extended family is not at the center of a Dane's life, while a Muslim revolves around a family institution, so extended that it includes all 1.3 billion Muslims! The concept of community for Muslims is unique: they think of each other as 'brothers and sisters' so some may get so heatedly angry in defense of 'brothers' they have never met, let alone that deeply loved and revered father-figure at the head of the family, namely Prophet Muhammad. How would any of us feel if his father was unjustly insulted in public? What will the reaction be if it continued for months?

⇨ This information is an extract of an article, reprinted with permission from Kwintessential. Visit www.kwintessential.co.uk for more information.

Hottest online brands in 2006

Information from Nielsen/NetRatings

Nielsen//NetRatings, the leading provider of internet research, today reveals the fastest growing online brands in the UK during 2006. The biggest web success stories of the year so far concern user-generated content and confirm Web 2.0 as the new phenomenon in the online world.

Generating and sharing content – the user in charge.

The three fastest growing online brands in the UK highlight how generating and sharing content is this year's online theme. YouTube, Flickr and MySpace all focus on technologies that allow users to define the content that their peers are looking at online. Factor in Photobucket, the photo and video sharing website, and social network Bebo and half of the ten fastest growing brands fall under the 'Web 2.0' umbrella.

Alex Burmaster, European Internet Analyst, comments,

'Last year indicated the potential for sites utilising the internet as a method for users to communicate and share information and the first half of 2006 has confirmed this. The idea of the user in charge through these so-called "Web 2.0" technologies is now a reality. The audience to video sharing phenomenon YouTube is testament to this, having grown by a factor of almost five during the year, meaning that more than one in eight Britons online now visit this site.

'Women currently make up 46% of the UK online population so brands such as Bebo and Odeon in particular tend to have a greater affinity with women than the internet as a whole. Conversely PhotoBucket, YouTube and American Express tend to "under-perform" on the female audience. Furthermore, Mozilla, producers of the Firefox web browser which competes with Microsoft's Internet Explorer are almost three times less likely to be visited by women compared to the entire UK internet audience.'

Note:
The growth information contained in this release compares the Unique Audience of brands in January 2006 and July 2006 and is based on the UK audience only.

⇨ This information was released by Nielsen/NetRatings on 14 September 2006. Visit www.nielsen–netratings.com for more information.

© *Nielsen/NetRatings*

The hottest online brands in 2006

Top 10 brands in 2006 by UK Unique Audience (UA) growth

Rank	Brand	UA % Growth Jan-Jul 2006	UA (000's) Jul 2006	Nature of Business
1	YouTube	478%	3,585	Video sharing
2	Flickr	131%	1,008	Photo management and sharing
3	MySpace	98%	3,502	Social networking
4	American Express	97%	1,178	Financial services
5	Photobucket	91%	838	Image/video hosting and sharing
6	Mozilla	91%	1,202	Web browsing software
7	Vodafone	86%	1,340	Telecommunications
8	Bebo	85%	2,784	Social networking
9	Odeon	82%	985	Cinemas
10	B&Q	72%	1,370	Home and garden retail

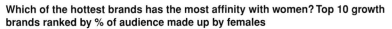

Which of the hottest brands has the most affinity with women? Top 10 growth brands ranked by % of audience made up by females

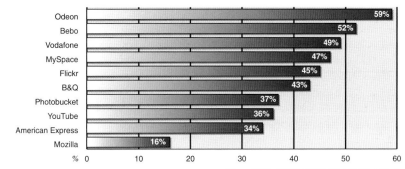

Brand	%
Odeon	59%
Bebo	52%
Vodafone	49%
MySpace	47%
Flickr	45%
B&Q	43%
Photobucket	37%
YouTube	36%
American Express	34%
Mozilla	16%

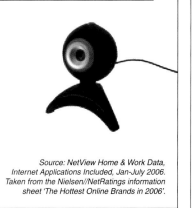

Source: NetView Home & Work Data, Internet Applications Included, Jan-July 2006. Taken from the Nielsen//NetRatings information sheet 'The Hottest Online Brands in 2006'.

Social networking

Social networking areas are basically websites with applications which help connect friends using a number of tools like blogs, profiles, internal email systems and photos

Well-known sites include Bebo, Myspace, Friendster and LiveJournal and have become an influential part of contemporary culture.

So – how do you use them?

Firstly, you sign up and create your own profiles or 'space'. Often, these contain standard blurbs like About Me and Who I'd Like to Meet and also include things like Music, Films, Sports, Scared Of and Happiest When. You can add specific personal details such as marital status, physical appearance, and the school you go to. You can also have your own blog where you can write daily thoughts or include articles you find interesting.

A big part of customising your 'space' can be uploading images or pictures onto your site. One of your pictures can be chosen to be the 'default image' and this will be seen on your profile's main page and as the image that will appear to the side of your user-name on comments, messages, etc.

Most sites also have a 'count' of the friends you have. A total of four, eight, twelve, or sixteen friends can be shown directly on the profile, with a link to a page which lists all of the user's friends. The 'Top Friends' list often becomes a touchy subject though, since it forces you to choose between friends which can sometimes be influenced by showing up on someone else's area!

You can sometimes also add music to your profile either by visiting an artist's page and choosing a song from their music player, or using a customised music player or embedded media file. There is often also an option to upload videos as well – including music videos and personally recorded films.

Stay in control:
There are a number of things to think about when using social networking sites
Be careful what information you

give out...
Be careful what information you give out on your profile, blog and through the images you post. Remember that you don't know who your friend's friends are… or your friend's friends' friends! And you don't know what they'll do with your picture or your phone number if you inadvertently give it out. Use a nickname or your initials on your profile – you don't want just anyone knowing your name.

Think through who you want to chat to...

Think through who you want to chat to, and how many of your personal thoughts you want anyone to view. Sometimes, it can seem a good idea to share what you got up to with your boyfriend last night, or the argument you had with your best mate; but as you're writing – remember that information could be public forever! Test yourself by asking 'would I want my teacher/Mum/Dad/ stranger on the train to see this?!' If the answer's no… don't post it!

Be careful who you agree to accept...

Be careful who you agree to accept into your forums / private chat areas. Unfortunately because there are so many young people using these sites – adults with bad intentions will use them to make contact with children too; so you're safer to only chat to people you know in the real world. Even if you know someone… who knows someone… who knows a person – unless you do; it's better to keep it that way!

Know where to go for help...

If you feel anyone is being weird with you or your friends; or if someone is bullying you on one of these sites – contact the administrator of the area. If it's really serious – like you think the person contacting you may be an adult who wants to abuse you or your mates – report on this site using the reporting button.

Things to think through:

⇨ Only upload pictures that you'd be happy for your mum to see – anything too sexy to be passed round the dinner table should NOT make it on to the web, as it could encourage sex-pests to contact you.

⇨ Don't post your phone number or email address on your homepage. Think about it – why would anyone actually need this info when they can message you privately via Myspace or Bebo?

⇨ Don't post pictures of you or your mates wearing school uniform – if dodgy people see your school badge, they can work out where you are and come and find you.

⇨ Adjust your account settings so only approved friends can instant message you. This won't ruin your social life – new people can still send you friend requests and message you, they just won't be able to pester you via IM.

⇨ Tick the 'no pic forwarding' option on your Myspace settings page – this will stop people sending pictures from your page around the world without your consent.

⇨ Don't give too much away in a blog. Yes, tell the world you're going to a party on Saturday night. But don't post details of where it is. Real friends can phone you to get details, and strangers shouldn't be able to see this kind of information.

⇨ This information is reprinted with permission from the Child Exploitation and Online Protection Centre. Visit www.thinkuknow.co.uk for more information.

Blogaholics anonymous?

Catherine Elsworth has been in Los Angeles covering the west coast of America for the *Daily Telegraph*

Several of my friends have recently voiced concerns about the amount of time they spend reading blogs. I've been on the verge of suggesting remedies – work in a place with no internet connection, set yourself a daily time limit then rip out the cable – when it occurs to me that, being the author of one of the gazillion vying for attention, this could prove counterproductive.

The dilemma does raise some valid questions, though, including how much blog time is too much? Chances are, if you read one blog, you read many. There are an estimated 70 million out there and most reference and link to a myriad more so clicking on one takes you to another and another and so forth. Soon you're deep in a maze of subtly-related sites with no ball of string to find your way out. It's lucky you can just close the browser.

Like food, blogs fall into different groups. There are the 'good ones', the wholegrains of the blogging world which are edifying and informative and leave you feeling virtuous (many news-based blogs and those by my *Telegraph* colleagues, for example).

Then there are the chips and Mars bars equivalents, the gossip-filled celebrity sites that deal in the same compelling qualms-free voyeurism of *Heat* and *Big Brother*. There are also several million that fall somewhere in between, delightful distractions such as Geoffrey's Chaucer's blog, that while certainly clever and entertaining probably wouldn't impress your boss.

Some of my friends with self-diagnosed 'blog issues' worry they devour too many 'bad' and not enough 'good' blogs and put themselves on corrective (i.e. 'celebrity-free') diets to weed out the junk. Others fear they spend too much time reading blogs full stop and try to work somewhere without internet connection, though this can prove counterproductive when so much of modern work requires access to email and the web.

According to health professionals, there is such a thing as too much blog time. Speaking to experts recently about so-called internet addiction, it was interesting to hear 'onlineaholism' described as being as dangerous as drug dependency or alcoholism. Many net addicts were risking their health, careers and relationships, experts such as Dr Hilarie Cash, founder of internet/Computer Addiction Services in Redmond, Washington, told me.

Blog addicts are a small but growing subset of internet addicts. Others compulsively surf news or sports websites, spend hours in chat-rooms or are unable to stop playing online games.

Dr Cash, whose website asks surfers if they are 'Feeling trapped by your computer?', offers help to those who simply turn off, embracing treatment techniques similar to the 12-step programme pioneered by Alcoholics Anonymous. (Those behind the Central Vermont Blog Addiction Treatment Centre have a slightly different take on the issue – their annual intake is held on 1st April.)

Blog authors, meanwhile, are encountering another problem – that updating blogs can prove an arduous bind.

Blogger Sarah Hepola recently pulled the plug on her five-year-old blog after reaching the conclusion it was actually an elaborate form of procrastination that prevented her from writing the book she'd always wanted to. 'I suspect I'll come back to blogging eventually. It will be something I quit on occasion, like whiskey and melted cheese, when the negative effects outweigh the benefits,' she writes, equating terminating a blog to switching off a mobile phone and not checking e–mails 'so that we can actually focus on something'.

Blog addicts who find it harder to quit can for now draw comfort from a case in New York where a judge handed the lightest sentence possible to a man accused of too much web browsing in office hours. The judge ruled that surfing the internet at work was no worse than reading a newspaper or talking on the phone.

Meanwhile, if you are an addict, apologies for contributing to your problem.

⇨ This article first appeared on telegraph.co.uk on 26 April 2006.
© *Telegraph Group Limited*

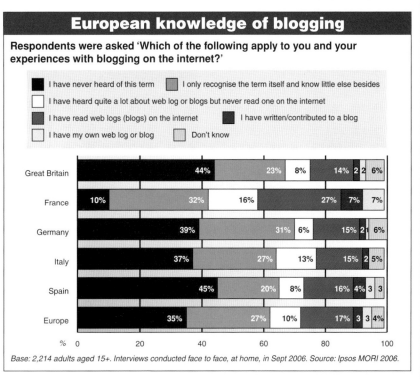

European knowledge of blogging

Respondents were asked 'Which of the following apply to you and your experiences with blogging on the internet?'

- ■ I have never heard of this term
- ▨ I only recognise the term itself and know little else besides
- □ I have heard quite a lot about web log or blogs but never read one on the internet
- ▨ I have read web logs (blogs) on the internet
- ■ I have written/contributed to a blog
- □ I have my own web log or blog
- ▨ Don't know

Great Britain	44%	23%	8%	14%	2 2	6%
France	10%	32%	16%	27%	7%	7%
Germany	39%	31%	6%	15%	2 1	6%
Italy	37%	27%	13%	15%	2	5%
Spain	45%	20%	8%	16%	4% 3	3
Europe	35%	27%	10%	17%	3 3	4%

% 0   20   40   60   80   100

Base: 2,214 adults aged 15+. Interviews conducted face to face, at home, in Sept 2006. Source: Ipsos MORI 2006.

The 'networked generation' finds TV is a turn-off

By David Derbyshire

Young adults are watching less television than they were four years ago, according to research published yesterday.

The lure of the internet, mobile phones and computer games means that those aged between 16 and 24 watch an hour and a half less television every week.

The fall in interest among younger viewers comes at a time when the average person is watching more TV than ever before.

Younger people also say that the internet has reduced their appetite for radio, magazines and newspapers.

The changing habits of the so-called 'networked generation' emerged from the annual report by Ofcom, the telecoms regulator.

It found that unlike older generations, who remain loyal to the traditional terrestrial broadcasters, younger viewers are being turned off by the main five channels.

They spend just 58 per cent of their viewing time watching BBC1, BBC2, ITV1, Channel 4 and Five. Four years ago the figure was 70 per cent.

Rather than spending their evenings slumped in front of the television, they are getting their entertainment from other sources.

They use their mobile phones far more than average, making 27 calls a week and sending 70 text messages. The typical Briton makes 20 calls and sends 28 texts.

They are also far more likely to listen to iPods and other portable music players, play games consoles and watch television on their computers than older people.

However, they are less likely to use Teletext or video recorders, both regarded by the young as outdated technology.

Although the report found little difference in the amount of internet use between younger and older people, it found that young people use the internet in a completely different way.

The report highlighted the popularity of 'social networking sites' such as Bebo and Myspace, where users can leave information about themselves and post messages to friends.

More than 70 per cent of 16–24-year-olds said they used a social networking site compared with 41 per cent of other adult users. More than half visited the sites at least once a week, compared with just 19 per cent of 25–34-year-olds and 10 per cent of people aged 35–44.

Twentyseven per cent of young adults said that since first using the internet they had read fewer newspapers, while 15 per cent said they had listened to less radio.

Ed Richards, Ofcom's chief operating officer, said the findings did not signal the death of any particular medium.

'It is an adjustment as a new medium, the internet, becomes more significant in people's lives,' he said.

The report also found that the five main terrestrial channels have been losing audience share in homes where multichannel television was available.

However, the rise in popularity of terrestrial spin-offs such as BBC3, BBC4 and ITV2 had more than compensated for the viewers lost by traditional channels.

⇨This article first appeared in The Telegraph on 11 August 2006.

© Telegraph Group Limited

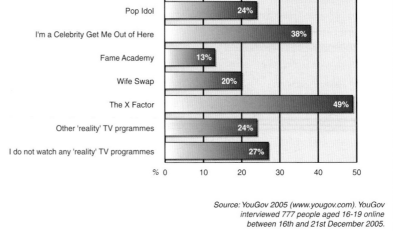

Young people and reality TV

Respondents were asked 'Do you watch any of the following TV programmes?'

Programme	%
Big Brother	49%
Pop Idol	24%
I'm a Celebrity Get Me Out of Here	38%
Fame Academy	13%
Wife Swap	20%
The X Factor	49%
Other 'reality' TV prgrammes	24%
I do not watch any 'reality' TV programmes	27%

% 0   10   20   30   40   50

Source: YouGov 2005 (www.yougov.com). YouGov interviewed 777 people aged 16-19 online between 16th and 21st December 2005.

Gaytime TV

Lindsey McQuitty turns her attention to the ongoing struggle that the marginalised gay and lesbian community face when trying to have their voices heard on mainstream television.

A lot of people, especially young people, watch television programmes where issues concerning homosexuality and lesbianism are an integral part of the storyline or indeed the actual focus of it.

I think that it's about time that there were more programmes like *Sugar Rush* and the *L Word* on mainstream television. Programmes like this have really helped to bring issues for the gay and lesbian community out of the closet and to finally make a positive contribution to our understanding of this often marginalised section of society.

Some people do not consider these sorts of programmes to be entertaining, informative or indeed educational. Instead they believe that it is a 'disgrace' for broadcasters to give airtime to gays and lesbians. Although everyone is entitled to their own opinion, these people would do well to consider that all sections of society have an equal right to be heard. Just as more mainstream opinions deserve to be heard so too do those of people who might be considered a minority. All opinions should be treated with equal respect. The viewer or listener should be given the chance to make up their own mind and not dictated to about what they can and can't watch.

After all, homosexuals watch programmes about the lives of heterosexual people and the way they live. It's about time that they were afforded the opportunity to watch programmes about their own community and issues affecting them. It's also about time that everyone else opened their minds and accepted diversity in our society and celebrated differences.

These types of programmes allow people to express their emotions about their sexuality and to educate others about those emotions. This kind of programme doesn't only make us laugh and cry but also shows us the sorts of issues that gays and lesbians face every day. These programmes show us all the same the love and heartbreak that heterosexuals encounter in their lives. After all love is the same no matter who you are and the effects of heartbreak are the same no matter who you are.

Young people who are trying to understand issues of sexuality can use shows like *Sugar Rush* to help them understand. As well as being of an educational value, programmes like like *Sugar Rush* and *The L Word* are highly entertaining.

These shows just don't teach the world about the gay and lesbian community, they also make use laugh, cry and also open up our minds to the choices that other people face in life. I think that television programmes for and about homosexuals are an entertainment genre in their own right and I think we are all much better of because of their inclusion in our television diet. Long may it continue to be so.

⇨   This information is reprinted with permission from Headliners. Visit www.headliners.org for more information.

© *Headliners*

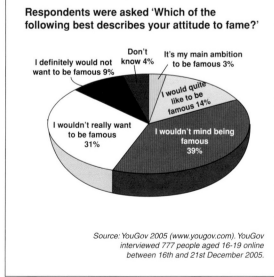

Young people and fame

Respondents were asked 'Which of the following best describes your attitude to fame?'

- Don't know 4%
- It's my main ambition to be famous 3%
- I definitely would not want to be famous 9%
- I would quite like to be famous 14%
- I wouldn't really want to be famous 31%
- I wouldn't mind being famous 39%

Source: YouGov 2005 (www.yougov.com). YouGov interviewed 777 people aged 16-19 online between 16th and 21st December 2005.

⇨ There are growing restrictions on the use of new media, brought about by the increasing volume and sophistication of communications. (page 1)

⇨ The publisher of the Harry Potter books threatened newspapers with legal action if they revealed details of the plot before the book's publication date. (page 3)

⇨ The Communications Act 2003 requires Ofcom to investigate matters of public interest arising from the merger of newspapers or broadcast media companies, should such an investigation be requested by the Secretary of State. (page 4)

⇨ More than two-thirds of people surveyed agree that 'the BBC is a national institution we should be proud of', but less than a third were happy with how it is funded. (page 6)

⇨ Some illegal radio stations attract a substantial audience, with 16% of adults in Greater London regularly listening to them. (page 7)

⇨ Under the Wireless Telegraphy Act 2006, it is illegal to broadcast without a licence and under the Communications Act 2003, Ofcom is responsible for keeping spectrum free from interference. (page 7)

⇨ UK newspapers are generally grouped into three groups – mass market tabloids, or red–tops (eg The Sun), middle–market tabloids (eg the Daily Mail), and quality broadsheets (eg The Times). (page 8)

⇨ Journalists should seek permission from an appropriate adult (parent/guardian/ teacher/ supervisor) before interviewing OR taking pictures of a child or young person (under 16). (page 11)

⇨ The reporter's job is to ask questions, but you are NOT obliged to answer them, especially if it involves revealing personal information you would prefer to keep private. (page 11)

⇨ The Freedom of Information Act (2000) came into force on 1 January, 2005. (page 17)

⇨ The FOI gives you the right to ask any public body for all the information they have on any subject you choose. Unless there's a good reason, the organisation must provide the information within a month. You can also ask for all the personal information they hold on you. (page 18)

⇨ If you request information about the environment it cannot be refused just because of what it would cost the public authority to comply. (page 19)

⇨ In the first quarter of 2005, more than a third of all requests to government departments (36%) took longer than the Act's 20 working day deadline to answer. (page 20)

⇨ The law recognises 'a vital public interest' in the protection of a journalist's sources. (page 22)

⇨ The media should not publish misleading information, including modified pictures, according to the UK Press Complaints Commission's Code of Practice. (page 24)

⇨ If the media publish a false story, people mentioned can take the company to court for libel or slander. Slander is when things have been said about someone that aren't true, for example in a TV report. Libel is when untrue things are printed in a newspaper or magazine. (page 26)

⇨ If a journalist reports allegations about public figures responsibly and the allegations are in the public interest, they will not be prosecuted under English law. (page 27)

⇨ There are guidelines on how sexual material should be covered in magazines targeted at teenagers. (page 28)

⇨ Journalists need to take care when reporting on suicides to reduce the risk of copycat behaviour. (page 30)

⇨ Ofcom found that while news helps just under half (43 per cent) of people feel part of the democratic process, almost as many (37 per cent) claimed that TV news puts them off politics. (page 31)

⇨ Young people and minority groups were less likely to be engaged with news. (page 32)

⇨ User-generated content is a theme of the fastest growing brands on the internet. (page 35)

⇨ New technologies mean that young people are watching less TV, even though older people are watching more than ever before. (page 38)

GLOSSARY

Arbitrate
To resolve a dispute between other parties.

Bandwidth
A range of frequencies that can transmit a signal.

Bias
An opinion or perspective that stops someone from being impartial.

Blog
Short for weblog; an online public journal.

Broadcast frequency:
Electronic waves used for transmission of information.

Censorship
Deliberate restrictions on printed or broadcast media or public speech, generally for political reasons.

Consolidation
Legal combination of two or more corporations to create a new corporation.

Convergence
Reduction in diversity; consolidation of communications into one network.

Defamation
Legal offence of writing or saying things that damage someone's reputation.

Democracy
Political system in which people elect their representatives.

FM
Frequency modulation; a way of encoding information in electronic waves.

Free press
Press not restricted or controlled by government censorship.

Freedom of expression
The right to speak or publish freely without fear of punishment.

Freedom of information
The right to access information.

Impartiality
Objectivity; giving equal weight to different perspectives and opinions.

Jargon
Specialised language relevant only in certain industries or professions.

Libel
Written defamation that causes harm to another person.

Licensing
A contractual agreement in which the person or organisation owning intellectual property for something (such as a story) allows another to use it.

Mass media
Media targeted at a large audience.

Misrepresentation
Knowingly presenting misleading or false information.

Ofcom
The UK media regulator.

Paparazzi
Photographers who take intrusive photos of celebrities.

Photojournalism
Presenting a story through images.

Proprietary system
A system that is developed and owned by an individual or organisation.

Public interest
Matters that will benefit people if made public, such as exposing criminal behaviour, protecting health or uncovering misrepresentation.

Socio-economic group AB
Professional and managerial people.

Socio-economic group DE
Poorly skilled and unemployed people.

Streaming
Playing video or sound at the same time it's being downloaded from the internet.

Telecommunications
Communications transmitted using the telephone network.

INDEX

Additional Resources

Other Issues titles

If you are interested in researching further some of the issues raised in *Media Issues*, you may like to read the following titles in the **Issues** series:

⇨ Vol. 121 *The Censorship Debate*
(ISBN 978 1 86168 354 0)

⇨ Vol. 104 *Our Internet Society*
(ISBN 978 1 86168 324 3)

⇨ Vol. 131 *Citizenship and National Identity*
(ISBN 978 1 86168 377 9)

For more information about these titles, visit our website at www.independence.co.uk/publicationslist

Useful organisations

You may find the websites of the following organisations useful for further research:

⇨ Campaign for Freedom of Information: www.cfoi.org.uk

⇨ Headliners: www.headliners.org

⇨ MediaUK: www.mediauk.com

⇨ MediaWise: www.mediawise.org.uk

⇨ National Union of Journalists: www.nuj.org.uk

⇨ Ofcom (Office of Communications): www.ofcom.org

ACKNOWLEDGEMENTS

The publisher is grateful for permission to reproduce the following material.

While every care has been taken to trace and acknowledge copyright, the publisher tenders its apology for any accidental infringement or where copyright has proved untraceable. The publisher would be pleased to come to a suitable arrangement in any such case with the rightful owner.

Chapter One: Control

New media regulation and convergence, © GreenNet Educational Trust, *The media,* © Expresso Broadband Limited, *UK media frozen out for new Potter,* © Guardian Newspapers Ltd, *Ofcom announces guidance on media mergers public interest test,* © Ofcom, *Parliament to decide whether media ownership has affected news,* © Press Gazette, *BBC funding debate,* © Moustrap Media, *Illegal broadcasting in the UK,* © Ofcom, *An introduction to newspapers in the UK,* © MediaUK, *Using the media,* © YouthNet, *Talking to journalists,* © MediaWise, *How can young people get their voices heard more in the media?,* © YouthNet, *Blair backs new online journalism register,* © Telegraph Group Limited.

Chapter Two: Accountability

Regional papers making good use of FOI, report shows, © holdthefrontpage.co.uk, *Freedom of information,* © Crown copyright, *'Unacceptable' freedom of information delays,* © Campaign for Freedom of Information, *Two-year FOI battle over 'Donnygate' quiz ends in victory for the Star,* © holdthefrontpage.co.uk, *Protection of sources upheld in High Court,* © National Union of Journalists, *Royal scoop too hot to handle,* © Pinsent Masons, *Reuters reacts to doctored photos,* © Pinsent Masons, *A snap too far,* © Headliners, *Media responsibility and personal privacy,* © Expresso Broadband Limited, *Journalists given new freedom under libel law,* © Simon Moore, *Teenage magazines, a responsible medium,* © Teenage Magazine Arbitration Panel, *The role of teenage magazines in the sexual health of young people,* © Teenage Magazine Arbitration Panel, *Do lads' mags teach young men about sex and relationships?,* © Dr Petra Boynton.

Chapter Three: Impact

Suicide coverage: time to take stock, © MediaWise, *New news, future news,* © Ofcom, *Cross cultural analysis of the Danish Prophet Muhammad cartoons,* © Kwintessential, *Hottest online brands in 2006,* © Nielsen/NetRatings, *Social networking,* © Child Exploitation and Online Protection Centre, *Blogaholics anonymous?,* © Telegraph Group Limited, *The 'networked generation' finds TV is a turn–off,* © Telegraph Group Limited, *Gaytime TV,* © Headliners

Illustrations and Photos:

P1: Cobi Smith; p3: Simon Kneebone; p4 and 5: Don Hatcher; p11: ItzaFineDay; p12: Jon Wisbey; p13: Prince Roy; p15 and 16: Angelo Madrid; p17 and 19: Don Hatcher; p20, Angelo Madrid; p21: Simon Kneebone; p22: Don Hatcher; p23: Simon Kneebone; p24: Angelo Madrid; p25, Simon Kneebone; p29: Bobbie Johnson, p31: Simon Kneebone.

Graphs

All graphs by Lisa Firth.

And with thanks to the team: Mary Chapman, Sandra Dennis and Jan Haskell.

Cobi Smith and Sophie Crewdson
Cambridge
September, 2007